Madeline &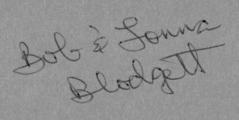

What a great example
you are to all of us!
We are sure that you
two could write your
own book on this
subject of "Love".

Bob & Jonna
Blodgett

LOVE
NOTES

LOVE
NOTES

A RANDOM REFERENCE
FOR THE MODERN ROMANTIC

Amy Maniatis, Elizabeth Weil,

and

Natasha Bondy

Literary Consultant: Al Alvarez

CHRONICLE BOOKS
SAN FRANCISCO

Library of Congress Cataloging-in-Publication Data available.
ISBN: 0-8118-4963-5
Manufactured in China.
DESIGNED BY SAM POTTS INC.

Distributed in Canada by Raincoast Books
9050 Shaughnessy Street
Vancouver, British Columbia V6P 6E5

10   9   8   7   6   5   4   3   2   1

Chronicle Books LLC
85 Second Street
San Francisco, California 94105
www.chroniclebooks.com

CONTENTS

CONTENTS *continued*

CONTENTS *continued*

INTRODUCTION

Falling in love—an affliction, an illness, a temporary or long lasting state of mind. Poets, anthropologists, psychologists, astrologists, and mystics have dedicated lifetimes to trying to explain this incredible phenomenon we hope we are all lucky enough to experience.

And so *Love Notes*. We had just finished writing a book, *Crib Notes*, that dealt with the major life transition of having a child, when our friend Natasha Bondy, a world class expert on love and passion and a BBC director asked the question: why not the same book on love? A book that covers everything and anything about the topic, taking advantage of what all those poets and scientists have learned over the years? Once that seed had taken root, the possibilities were endless. We began to remember favorite songs, famous couples, indelible moments from films. Whenever we mentioned the book to friends, the ideas poured forth. No one can remain silent on the subject of love.

So here is our "little black book" on love, a reference to celebrate the highs and lows and a companion for moments of reflection. On our best days, love is at the center of our lives. We hope you're as inspired by what's on these pages as we are.

CLINICAL SYMPTOMS OF
LOVE SICKNESS

Obsessive thoughts

Erratic mood swings

Insomnia

Loss of appetite

Recurrent and persistent images and impulses
(irresistible urges to phone or text)

Superstitious or ritualistic compulsions
(she loves me, she loves me not)

Inability to concentrate

Delusion

HOW TO CHOOSE A DIAMOND

THE FOUR Cs: CUT, COLOR, CLARITY, AND CARATS

CUT: This is the most important characteristic of a diamond because it determines how much of the light that enters a diamond is reflected back—in other words, how much a diamond sparkles. In a badly cut diamond, all the light will be reflected out the sides and the bottom instead of bouncing out the top. The deep cut diamond reflects the most light out the top.

| SHALLOW CUT | DEEP CUT | IDEAL CUT |

COLOR: The best color for a diamond is no color at all. The Gemological Institute of America rates diamonds on a letter scale from D to Z. *Fancy* diamonds are colored diamonds—pink, yellow, blue, or red.

Scale	D	E	F	G	H	I	J	K	L	M	N	O	P	Q	R	S	T	U	V	W	X	Y	Z	Fancy
Color	Colorless			Near Colorless				Faint Yellow			Very Light Yellow					Light Yellow								Color

CLARITY: Most diamonds have flaws—tiny scratches, trace minerals—and the clarity scale grades their severity.

Scale	FL	IF	VVS^1	VVS^2	VS^1	VS^2	SI^1	SI^2	I^1	I^2	I^3
Clarity	Flawless-Internally Flawless		Very Very Slightly Imperfect		Very Slightly Imperfect		Slightly Imperfect		Imperfect		

CARATS: Diamonds are measured in a unit of mass called carats, not by size. One carat is equal to one-fifth of a gram. Because larger diamonds are far less common than smaller ones, value goes up exponentially with carat size.

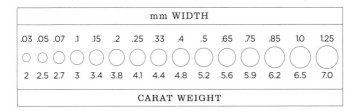

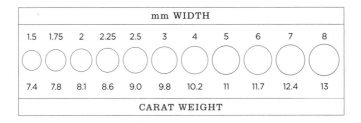

CHAT ROOM ACRONYMS
FOR LOVE AND ROMANCE

AML	All My Love
BF/GF	Boyfriend/Girlfriend
DH	Darling Husband
FYEO	For Your Eyes Only
GBH&K	Great Big Hug and Kisses
KOL	Kiss on the Lips
HAGN	Have a Good Night
HB	Hug Back
IHTFP	I Have Truly Found Paradise
II	I'm Impressed
IIT	I'm Impressed Too
ILY	I Love You
ILYFAE	I Love You Forever and Ever
IWALY	I Will Always Love You
K	Kiss
KB	Kiss Back
LYWAMH	Love You with All My Heart
OL/OM	Old Lady/Old Man (wife/husband)
QT	Cutie
SHMILY	See How Much I Love You?
TOY	Thinking of You
VBS	Very Big Smile
WYMM	Will You Marry Me?
YWTLM	You Want to Love Me
SO	Significant Other

爱

LOVE

欲望

LUST/DESIRE

永恒的爱

ETERNAL LOVE

我爱你

I LOVE YOU

心

HEART

漂亮的妻子

BEAUTIFUL WIFE

Rick: Where I'm going, you can't follow. What I've got to do, you can't be any part of. Ilsa, I'm no good at being noble, but it doesn't take much to see that the problems of three little people don't amount to a hill of beans in this crazy world. Someday you'll understand that. Now, now. Here's looking at you, kid.

Laszlo: Everything in order?

Rick: All except one thing. There's something you should know before you leave.

Laszlo: (sensing what is coming) Blaine, I don't ask you to explain anything.

Rick: I'm going to anyway, because it may make a difference to you later on. You said you knew about Ilsa and me.

Laszlo: Yes.

Rick: But you didn't know she was at my place last night when you were. She came there for the letters of transit. Isn't that true, Ilsa?

Ilsa: (facing Laszlo) Yes.

Rick: (forcefully) She tried everything to get them, and nothing worked. She did her best to convince me that she was still in love with me, but that was all over long ago. For your sake, she pretended it wasn't, and I let her pretend.

Laszlo: I understand.

Rick: Here it is. *(Rick hands the letters to Laszlo.)*

Laszlo: Thanks. I appreciate it. *(Laszlo extends his hand to Rick, who grasps it firmly.)* And welcome back to the fight. This time I know our side will win.

WHY MEN ARE MORE LIKELY
TO FALL IN LOVE AT FIRST SIGHT

Researcher Helen Fisher, together with her colleagues at Rutgers University, speculates that the visual response in men may cause them to fall in love "at first sight" more easily than women.

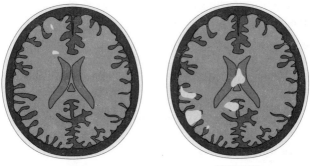

MEN   WOMEN

In the early stages of falling in love, MRI scans of women's brains show more activity in regions associated with memory, mental images, emotion, and attention, as well as the septum, or "pleasure center."

Scans of men's brains show more activity in the visual cortex and visual processing areas, including one area responsible for sexual arousal.

LINGERIE:
A GLOSSARY OF TERMS

Baby doll: A sleeveless, loose-fitting top or bra with sheer material attached. Lengths vary from just under the breasts to the derriere. Usually comes with a matching panty.

Bikini panty: Offers full coverage in both the front and back while the sides rest high on the hips or waist.

Brief: A full-coverage, to-the-waist panty, cut low on the thigh.

Bustier: A tight-fitting top; a bra with fitted sides that extend down the waist to provide an hourglass look.

Camisole, or cami: A short sleeveless lingerie top, fitted over the bust and extending to the waistline.

Charmeuse: A man-made, satinlike fabric.

Chemise: A sleep gown with no waistline, designed to fall flatteringly from the upper torso.

Chiffon: A sheer fabric made of silk, polyester, or other fibers.

Corset: Cinches in and defines the waist, with no shoulder straps.

G-string: A panty with a very thin, stringlike band of fabric in the back.

Garter belt: A garment that sits at the hip, with straps to hold up stockings.

Garter: Elastic strap with hook attachments that hang from the bottom of a bustier, teddy, or garter belt and used to hold up stockings.

Kimono: A robe with wide sleeves, traditionally worn with a broad sash as an outer garment.

Merry widow: A bustier with garters attached.

Marabou: Soft, feathery, fluffy material prepared from turkey feathers or the coverts of marabous and used for trimming in women's wear.

Tap pants: A very feminine boxer short, usually made from soft, sensual, silky, and/or sheer materials.

Teddy: A one-piece garment, like a bodysuit, usually strapless, often without garters.

Thong: A panty with a small strip or band of fabric in the back. Thongs have more material in the back than G-strings.

REEL TO REAL LOVE

ON-SCREEN TO OFF-SCREEN ROMANCES

MOVIE	REEL COUPLE	REAL COUPLE
Flesh and the Devil 1926	Leo von Harden & Felicitas	John Gilbert & Greta Garbo
Woman of the Year 1942	Sam Craig & Tess Harding	Spencer Tracy & Katharine Hepburn
To Have and Have Not 1944	Harry "Steve" Morgan & Marie "Slim" Browning	Humphrey Bogart & Lauren Bacall
Stromboli 1950	Ingrid Bergman as Karin, directed by Roberto Rossellini	Roberto Rossellini & Ingrid Bergman
Cleopatra 1963	Marc Antony & Cleopatra	Richard Burton & Elizabeth Taylor
The Getaway 1972	Carter "Doc" McCoy & Carol Ainsley McCoy	Steve McQueen & Ali MacGraw
Days of Thunder 1990	Cole Trickle & Dr. Claire Lewicki	Tom Cruise & Nicole Kidman
Proof of Life 2000	Terry Thorne & Alice Bowman	Russell Crowe & Meg Ryan
Daredevil 2003	Matt Murdock/Daredevil & Elektra Natchios	Ben Affleck & Jennifer Garner

SHAKESPEARE'S LOVERS
AND THEIR FATES

PLAY	LOVERS	FATE
Romeo and Juliet	Romeo & Juliet	Double suicide: Romeo takes poison, believing Juliet to be dead; Juliet stabs herself with his dagger.
Antony and Cleopatra	Antony & Cleopatra	Double suicide: Antony falls on his sword; Cleopatra is bitten by a poisonous snake.
As You Like It	Rosalind & Orlando	Rosalind and Orlando marry, but only after Rosalind has disguised herself as a boy and instructed Orlando in the art of courtship.
Twelfth Night	Orsino & Viola, Olivia & Sebastian	Orsino marries Viola and Olivia marries Sebastian, Viola's twin brother, also after much cross-dressing.
Much Ado About Nothing	Beatrice & Benedick	Beatrice and Benedick are tricked into marriage against their better judgment.
Othello	Othello & Desdemona	Othello murders his wife Desdemona, then kills himself.
A Winter's Tale	Perdita & Florizel	Perdita and Florizel, the most tender of all Shakespeare's young lovers, end up happily married.
The Tempest	Ferdinand & Miranda	Ferdinand and Miranda are last seen sailing off into the sunset, engaged to be married.

Snoring is an anatomical problem that occurs when the roof of the mouth (known as the soft palate) and the soft tissue at the back of the throat vibrate during sleep. The resulting sound is not unlike that produced by a balloon when the air is let out. In both cases, soft structures flap against each other, creating a loud fluttering noise.

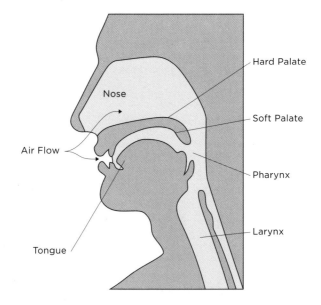

VICTORIAN FLIRTATION:
FANNING THE FLAMES

Courting in the Victorian era was an extremely complicated procedure. It was deemed inappropriate for young men and women to talk openly, let alone flirt with each other, so a more subtle way of communicating was devised. One of these was the use of the hand-held fans that ladies carried with them.

Over the years, each of the various flappings and fannings meant something different and pointed to the potential suitor.

Fan open wide ....Love

Fan drawn across the cheek ....I love you

Fan twirled in the right hand ....I love another

Fan half open ....Friendship

Fan fast ....I am independent

Fan slow ....I am engaged

Fan with right hand in front of face ....Come on

Fan with left hand in front of face ....Leave me

Fan open and shut ....Kiss me

Fan drawn through the hand ....I hate you

Drawing fan across forehead............................We are being watched

Presenting the fan closed.....................................Do you love me?

Letting fan rest on right cheek ....Yes

Letting fan rest on left cheek ....No

Pulling fan across the eyes ....I apologize

RECIPE FOR A
CHAMPAGNE COCKTAIL

from Jerry Thomas's *How to Mix Drinks* (1862)

1 cube sugar
Angostura bitters
6 ounces chilled champagne
Twist of lemon

Take a sugar cube and hold it over the opening of the Angostura bitters bottle. Tip the bottle slightly so some of the bitters soak in to the sugar cube.

Place the cube in to a champagne flute and pour in the champagne.

Finish with a little twist of lemon.

Over millions of years, human beings have developed funda-
mental instincts concerning attraction in order to further the
species.

Upside-down triangle   Women look for men with broad
shoulders and a narrow waist. This indicates great upper body
strength and a good immune system.

Waist-to-hip ratio   Men look for women with a waist to hip
ratio of 0.7, regardless of total body mass. Young girls and
older women tend to have ratios closer to 1.0. In girls, hips are
not yet developed, and in older women fat is stored around the
stomach. Both coincide with lack of fertility.

Symmetry   Both men and women are attracted to symmetrical faces. A symmetrical face indicates good health; an asym-
metrical one suggests underlying genetic problems. Women
show a stronger preference for symmetry than do men. This
is because women prioritize a man's ability to provide and
protect.

Pheromones   Humans are attracted to the pheromones, or
chemical scents, of people who are most *dissimilar* to themselves. This is for reproductive health: the greater the similar-
ity between two partners' genes, the greater the probability
that a resulting baby will have genetic problems.

COMPATIBLE ASTROLOGICAL SIGNS

	MOST COMPATIBLE	SOMEWHAT COMPATIBLE	LEAST COMPATIBLE	NEUTRAL
Aries 3/21–4/19	Leo, Sagittarius	Taurus, Gemini, Pisces, Aquarius	Cancer, Libra, Capricorn	Virgo, Scorpio
Taurus 4/20–5/20	Virgo, Capricorn	Gemini, Cancer, Pisces, Aries	Aquarius, Leo, Scorpio	Libra, Sagittarius
Gemini 5/21–6/21	Libra, Aquarius	Cancer, Leo, Aries, Taurus	Virgo, Sagittarius, Pisces	Scorpio, Capricorn
Cancer 6/22–7/22	Scorpio, Pisces	Leo, Virgo, Taurus, Gemini	Aries, Libra, Capricorn	Sagittarius, Aquarius
Leo 7/23–8/22	Sagittarius, Aries	Virgo, Libra, Gemini, Cancer	Scorpio, Aquarius, Taurus	Pisces, Capricorn
Virgo 8/23–9/22	Capricorn, Taurus	Libra, Scorpio, Leo, Cancer	Sagittarius, Pisces, Gemini	Aquarius, Aries
Libra 9/23–10/23	Aquarius, Gemini	Scorpio, Sagittarius, Leo, Virgo	Aries, Capricorn, Cancer	Pisces, Taurus
Scorpio 10/24–11/21	Pisces, Cancer	Sagittarius, Capricorn, Virgo, Libra	Aquarius, Taurus, Leo	Aries, Gemini
Sagittarius 11/22–12/21	Aries, Leo	Capricorn, Aquarius, Libra, Scorpio	Pisces, Gemini, Virgo	Taurus, Cancer
Capricorn 12/22–1/19	Taurus, Virgo	Aquarius, Pisces, Scorpio, Sagittarius	Aries, Cancer, Libra	Gemini, Leo
Aquarius 1/20–2/19	Gemini, Libra	Sagittarius, Capricorn, Pisces, Aries	Taurus, Leo, Scorpio	Cancer, Virgo
Pisces 2/20–3/20	Cancer, Scorpio	Capricorn, Aquarius, Aries, Taurus	Gemini, Virgo, Sagittarius	Leo, Libra

Catullus & Lesbia

Dante & Beatrice

Francesco Petrarch & Laura de Noves

John Donne & Anne Donne

John Keats & Fanny Brawne

Robert Schumann & Clara Schumann

Frederick Chopin & George Sand

D. H. Lawrence & Frieda von Richthofen

Sylvia Plath & Ted Hughes

Gustav Mahler & Alma Schindler

Walter Gropius & Alma Schindler

Franz Werfel & Alma Schindler

Samuel Johnson & Hester Thrale

Lewis Carroll & Alice Liddell

Dante Gabriel Rossetti & Elizabeth Siddal

Salvador Dalí & Gala Dalí

Man Ray & Lee Miller

Edward Weston & Charis Weston

George Balanchine & Suzanne Farrell

John Lennon & Yoko Ono

Andrew Wyeth & Helga Testorf

Pablo Picasso & Jacqueline Roque

F. Scott Fitzgerald & Zelda Fitzgerald

Henry Miller & Anaïs Nin

TRIANGULAR THEORY OF LOVE

Three key elements—intimacy, passion, and commitment—
form the triangle of love. Relationships based on a single ele-
ment are less likely to survive than ones based on two or more.
Couples with similar triangles tend to be more satisfied in their
relationships than couples with dissimilar triangles.

FORMS OF LOVE	ELEMENTS		
Romantic love	Intimacy	Passion	
Compassionate love			Decision/ Commitment
Fatuous love (Whirlwind romance)		Passion	Decision/ Commitment
Consummate love	Intimacy	Passion	Decision/ Commitment

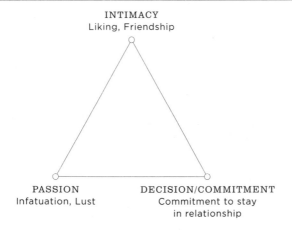

INTIMACY
Liking, Friendship

PASSION
Infatuation, Lust

DECISION/COMMITMENT
Commitment to stay
in relationship

SOME VEGAS "I DO'S"

COUPLE	YEAR
Mickey Rooney & Ava Gardner	1942
Betty Grable & Harry James (a musician)	1943
Zsa Zsa Gabor & George Sanders	1949
Rita Hayworth & Dick Haymes (singer)	1953
Kirk Douglas & Anne Buydens	1954
Joan Crawford & Alfred Steele (then chairman of the board of Pepsi-Cola)	1955
Paul Newman & Joanne Woodward	1958
Judy Garland & Mark Herron	1965
Jane Fonda & Roger Vadim	1965
Frank Sinatra & Mia Farrow	1966
Elvis Presley & Priscilla Anne Beaulieu	1967
Leslie Ann Warren & Jon Peters (her hairdresser)	1967
Diana Ross & Robert Silberstein	1971
George Hamilton & Alana Collins	1972
Michael Caine & Shakira Baksh	1973
David Cassidy & Kay Lenz (actress)	1977
Joan Collins & Peter Holm (singer)	1985
Bob Geldof & Paula Yates	1986
Demi Moore & Bruce Willis	1987
Dudley Moore & Brogan Lane	1988
Jon Bon Jovi & Dorothea Hurley	1989
Cindy Crawford & Richard Gere	1991
Noel Gallagher & Meg Matthews	1997
Angelina Jolie & Billy Bob Thornton	2000
Britney Spears & Jason Allen Alexander	2004

LAS VEGAS WEDDING CHAPELS

Aaron's Chapel of the Bells

A Hollywood Wedding
Chapel

A Las Vegas Wedding Chapel

A Little White Chapel

A San Francisco Sally's
Wedding Chapel

A Special Memory Wedding
Chapel

A Viva Las Vegas Wedding
Chapel

Bellagio Wedding Chapel

Caesars Palace Chapel

Candlelight Wedding Chapel

Canterbury Wedding Chapel

Chapel at Monte Carlo

Chapel by the Bay

Chapel of Love

Chapel of the Fountain

Chapel of Your Dreams

Chapelle de Paris

Cupid's Wedding Chapel

Divine Madness Fantasy
Wedding Chapel

Graceland Wedding Chapel

Flamingo Garden Chapel

Forever Grand Wedding
Chapel

Island Wedding Chapel

Little Chapel of the Flowers

Little Church of the West

Shalimar Wedding Chapel

Silver Bell Wedding Chapel

Sweethearts Wedding Chapel

Texas Station Wedding
Chapel

Victoria's Wedding Chapel

Wedding Bells Chapel

Wedding Chapel at the Rio

Wedding Chapels at
Treasure Island

"I'll Never Fall in Love Again"	*Dionne Warwick*
"What's Love Got to Do with It"	*Tina Turner*
"Love Stinks"	*The J. Geils Band*
"Love Don't Live Here Anymore"	*Rose Royce*
"Ever Fallen in Love (with Someone You Shouldn't Have Fallen in Love With)"	*The Buzzcocks*
"Love Hurts"	*Nazareth*
"Love Is a Battlefield"	*Pat Benatar*
"Where Is the Love?"	*Donnie Hathaway and Roberta Flack*
"I Can't Make You Love Me"	*Bonnie Raitt*
"I'm Not in Love"	*10cc*
"Love Will Tear Us Apart"	*Joy Division*
"Tainted Love"	*Soft Cell*
"You're So Vain"	*Carly Simon*
"50 Ways to Leave Your Lover"	*Paul Simon*
"Bye Bye Love"	*Everly Brothers*
"You Don't Own Me"	*Leslie Gore*
"Silver Threads and Golden Needles"	*Everly Brothers*
"That'll Be the Day"	*Buddy Holly*
"I Don't Need Love"	*Sammy Hagar*
"No More I-Love-You's"	*Annie Lennox*
"Don't Tell Me You Love Me"	*Night Ranger*
"You've Got to Hide Your Love Away"	*The Beatles*
"Lovin', Touchin', Squeezin'"	*Journey*
"The One I Love"	*R.E.M.*
"Love on the Rocks"	*Neil Diamond*

"Is That Love," "Goodbye Girl"	*Squeeze*
"You Wanted More," "Knock Down Walls," "Mean to Me"	*Tonic*
"I'm Looking through You"	*The Beatles*
"Thorn in My Side"	*Eurthymics*
"Over You," "End of the Line"	*Roxy Music*
"You Don't Bring Me Flowers"	*Barbara Streisand and Neil Diamond*
"Don't You Want Me"	*Human League*
"Train in Vain (Stand By Me)," "Lost in the Supermarket"	*The Clash*
"No Man's Woman"	*Sinead O'Connor*
"I'm Losing You," "Nobody Loves You When You're Down and Out"	*John Lennon*
"Will Never Marry"	*Morrissey*
"My Favorite Mistake"	*Sheryl Crow*
"Ain't It a Shame"	*The B-52's*
"Turn and Walk Away"	*Babys*
"Letters"	*Stroke 9*
"I Walk Alone"	*Oleander*
"The Crying Game"	*Boy George*
"Song for the Dumped"	*Ben Folds Five*
"Heaven Knows I'm Miserable Now," There's a Light That Never Goes Out"	*The Smiths*
"Let Down"	*Radiohead*
"Damn It"	*Blink-182*
"Miserable"	*Lit*

Married people live longer: single men have mortality rates 250 percent higher than married men; single women have mortality rates 50 percent higher than married women.

Married individuals have lower rates of alcoholism: single men drink twice as much as married men.

Married people are less likely to die from almost everything, including cancer, heart disease, stroke, car accidents, and murder.

Married individuals tend to have stronger immune systems, and so are less likely to develop colds and other illnesses than unmarried individuals.

Approximately 40 percent of married people have sex twice a week, compared to 20 to 25 percent of single or cohabiting men and women.

Married people tend to be happier than single people.

Married men are half as likely to commit suicide than single men.

Married persons are more likely to report feeling hopeful, happy, and good about themselves.

Married couples have higher incomes than single men and women.

Married men are more successful at work, getting promoted more often and receiving better reviews than their single counterparts.

SEX AND SPORTS ANALOGIES

Knockout

Play the field

Go short

First base

Second base

Third base

All the way

Home run

Score

Make a pass

Foreplay

Stop short

Play skins

Take one for the team

Strike out

Hit and run

Block the box

Give the Heisman

Slip one past the goalie

Pull the goalie

Wingman

Play for both teams

Switch hit

Split the uprights

Shoot through the five-hole

He shoots, he scores

"To love someone deeply gives you strength. Being loved by someone deeply gives you courage."

>—*Lao-tzu* (c. 570–490 B.C.), Chinese philosopher, founder of Taoism

"By all means marry; if you get a good wife, you'll become happy; if you get a bad one, you'll become a philosopher."

>—*Socrates* (469–399 B.C.), Greek philosopher

"Love is a grave mental disease."

>—*Plato* (427–347 B.C.), Greek philosopher and student of Socrates

"That which men desire they are said to love, and to hate those things for which they have aversion. So that desire and love are the same thing; save that by desire, we signify the absence of the object; by love, most commonly the presence of the same."

>—*Thomas Hobbes* (1588–1679), English philosopher

"Love is nothing but a pleasurable state, joy, accompanied by the idea of an external cause."

>—*Baruch Spinoza* (1632–77), Dutch philosopher

"If you marry, you will regret it; if you don't marry, you will also regret it."

>—*Søren Kierkegaard* (1813–55), Dutch philosopher

"To write a good love letter, you ought to begin without knowing what you mean to say, and to finish without knowing what you have written."

> —*Jean-Jacques Rousseau* (1712–78), French writer and political theorist

"If married couples did not live together, happy marriages would be more frequent."

> —*Friedrich Nietzsche* (1844–1900), German existentialist

"Man makes love by braggadocio and woman makes love by listening."

> —*H. L. Mencken* (1880–1956), American literary critic, journalist, and essayist

"Love is the only sane and satisfactory answer to the problem of human existence."

> —*Erich Fromm* (1900–80), German philosopher

"It is love, and not German philosophy, that is the true explanation of this world, whatever may be the explanation of the next."

> —*Oscar Wilde* (1854–1900), Irish writer

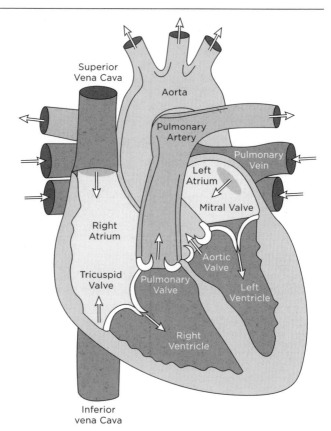

Superior
Vena Cava

Aorta

Pulmonary
Artery

Pulmonary
Vein

Left
Atrium

Mitral Valve

Right
Atrium

Aortic
Valve

Tricuspid
Valve

Pulmonary
Valve

Left
Ventricle

Right
Ventricle

Inferior
vena Cava

SOME FAMOUS LOVERS IN MYTH, HISTORY, AND FICTION

Helen of Troy & Paris

Troilus & Cressida

Theseus & Ariadne

Dido & Aeneas

Antony & Cleopatra

Eloise & Abelard

Sir Lancelot & Queen Guinevere

Romeo & Juliet

Beatrice & Benedick

Florizel & Perdita

Ferdinand & Miranda

Othello & Desdemona

Elizabeth Bennett & Mr. Darcy

Jane Eyre & Mr. Rochester

Heathcliff & Catherine

Anna Karenina & Vronsky

Prince Andrew Bolkonsky & Natasha Rostova

Dr. Zhivago & Lara

Leda & the Swan

Pasiphaë & the Bull

Portnoy & the Monkey

TRADITIONAL WEDDING RESPONSIBILITIES

(WHO PAYS FOR WHAT)

BRIDE

Bridesmaids' lodging

Bridesmaids' gifts

Couple's stationery and
thank-you notes

Wedding programs and
guest book

BRIDE'S FAMILY

Engagement and wedding
pictures

Invitations

Wedding dress

Wedding consultant

Ceremony fees

Flowers

Bridesmaids' bouquets and
fathers' boutonnieres

Reception

Music for ceremony, cocktail
hour, and reception

Bridesmaids' luncheon

Transportation for bridal
party to ceremony and
reception

BRIDESMAIDS

Bridal shower

Bridesmaid dress and shoes

Bachelorette party

GROOM

Engagement ring

Marriage license

Officiant's fee

Formal wear

Groomsmen's lodging

Groomsmen's gifts

Boutonnieres for self and
groomsmen

Flowers for mothers and
grandmothers

Bride's bouquet

Wedding bands

Honeymoon

GROOM'S FAMILY

Rehearsal dinner

USHERS

Rental fees for formal wear

Bachelor party

AVERAGE WEDDING COSTS (U.S.)

Invitations, announcements, thank-you notes, etc.	$ 327
Bouquets and other flowers	$ 756
Photography and videography	$ 1,311
Music	$ 830
Clergy, church, chapel, synagogue fee	$ 232
Limousine	$ 393
Attendants' gifts	$ 308
Wedding rings (bride and groom)	$ 1,016
Engagement ring	$ 3,044
Rehearsal dinner	$ 698
Bride's wedding dress	$ 823
Bride's headpiece/veil	$ 166
Bridal attendants' apparel (five attendants)	$ 790
Mother of the bride's apparel	$ 231
Groom's formalwear (rented)	$ 95
Men's formalwear (ushers, best man)	$ 449
Wedding reception	$ 7,635
GRAND TOTAL	$ 19,104

BUILT FOR LOVE:
THE TAJ MAHAL

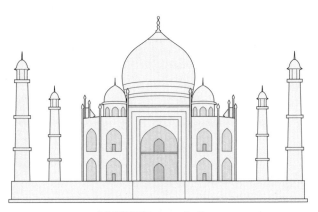

LOCATION: Agra, India

Built by Shah Jahan in the seventeenth-century in memory of his wife Mumtaz Mahal, who had died in childbirth at the age of thirty-nine.

The monument took twenty thousand workers twenty years to build.

SOME COUNTRY-AND-WESTERN
LOVE SONGS

"Get Your Tongue out of My Mouth 'cause I'm Kissing You Goodbye"

"If My Nose Were Running Money Honey, I'd Blow It All on You"

"How Can I Miss You If You Won't Go Away?"

"She Made Toothpicks of the Timber of My Heart"

"I Keep Forgettin' I Forgot About You"

"I'm So Miserable Without You, It's Like Having You Around"

"If You Leave Me, Can I Come Too?"

"If You Walk away from Me, I'll Love You from Behind"

"Lovin' here and Livin' there and Lyin' in Between"

"I Just Heard a Heart Break, I'm So Afraid It's Mine"

"You Can Lead a Heart to Love but You Can't Make It Fall"

"There's a Tear in My Beer Tonight"

"Don't Come Home a-Drinkin' with Lovin' on Your Mind"

TYPE (Love is like . . .)	TYPICAL VIEW OF RELATIONSHIPS	ADVANTAGES	DISADVANTAGES	POTENTIAL FOR SUCCESS
Art	" — is the most beautiful / handsome partner I could ever find."	Intense physical attraction. Concern for partner's well-being	When partner's looks start to go, uh-oh! Partner is loved for appearance and not for self.	Low if partner loses attractive personal appearance. Moderate while partner retains. High if couple is flexible and willing to modify the recipe over time.
Cookbook	"We succeed because we always . . ."	Belief that with the right recipe, the relationship will make a good story.	Rigidity. Incomprehension that no recipe fully guarantees success.	Moderate if couple is rigid. High if couple is flexible and willing to modify the recipe over time.
Fantasy	"He's my knight in shining armor." "She's my dream come true."	Admiration and respect for partner. Willingness to do a great deal to keep partner happy.	Lack of realism. Expectations that no one can fulfill.	Poor if person expects fantasy to continue forever. Good if tempered with realism.
Games & Sports	"I play to win."	Excitement. Sense of fun. Recognition that life should not always be taken seriously.	May not take relationship seriously. Goal may be to "win." May be competitive in relationship.	Variable. Not so good if gamelike aspects predominate. OK if gamelike aspects are just part of the relationship.
Gardening	"I tend to my relationship the way I would to a beautiful rose."	Partner is cared for. Relationship is "watered" continually.	"Overwatering." Lack of spontaneity.	Generally excellent.

Government	"I [my partner] am the one who makes the decisions on the relationship."	Recognition of the importance of power in relationships. If democratic, concern with sharing of power.	If autocratic, one partner seeks all real power for him or herself. Potential for becoming either tyrant or a slave.	Variable. Depends on whether person is democratic (excellent), autocratic (poor), or anarchic (poor).
House & Home	"Our home is the center of our life."	Recognition of the importance of having a comfortable living environment.	Maintenance of pretty home can become a substitute for a strong relationship. Too much emphasis on decoration.	Generally good.
Humor	"My wife ran away with my best friend and I really miss him" (and other funnies).	Sense of fun. Recognition that life has a funny side. Ability to see humor in tense situations.	May not take relationship seriously, or know how it should be taken seriously. May use humor to cover up problems.	Not so good if relationship is seen as or becomes a joke. Good if humor is just part of the relationship.
Mystery	"I have lots of secrets and I like it that way. It keeps him/her guessing."	Excitement and sense of constant need to know more about your partner. Adventure.	Partners never really get to know one another. Mystery may hide "double life." Lack of communication.	Good up to a point; not good if mystery hides fundamental facts about a person or his/her activities.
Religion	"Love is my salvation."	Intense devotion to partner. Love has important place in person's life.	Unrealistic expectation of what love can provide. Dogmatic views about what love is and can be.	Variable, depending on intensity. Poor if fanatical.
Travel	"We're always in the process of becoming."	Dynamism in relationships. Focus on the future. Planning for tomorrow.	In extreme, need for too much change.	Excellent.

According to Yale psychologist Robert Sternberg, the stories about love can predict their relationships's success.

THE PHYSIOLOGY OF DESIRE

The pupils dilate, a result of adrenaline and a sign of sexual interest.

Dopamine, the so-called "feel-good chemical," is released in the brain.

Pheromones, or chemical scents, are released in the sweat.

Adrenaline courses through the body.

Blood is redirected away from the stomach (giving the familiar feeling of "butterflies" in the stomach) and toward the lips and sexual organs.

TRADITIONAL WEDDING RINGS

GIMMEL RING

A gimmel ring is three separate rings worn together. The three rings symbolize the man, the woman, and the witness to the marriage. Before the wedding, the bride, groom, and witness each wear one of the rings, and only during the ceremony itself are all three put on the bride's finger for the first time.

POSY RING

Posy rings usually have an inscription inside, a motto or short poem like "To You I Will Always Be True" or "Let Love Increase." They may also have stones set in them, with the first letters of each stone's name spelling out a word, like Lapis, Opal, Verd Antique, and Emerald for *love*.

IRISH CLADDAGH

This ring is believed to have originated in the Claddagh, a small fishing community near Galway Bay. The design is a heart topped by a crown, held by two hands. The phrase usually associated with this ring is "Let Love and Friendship Reign."

WEDDING DRESS COLORS
DECODED

White ....You have chosen right.

Blue ....You will always be true.

Yellow ....Ashamed of your fellow.

Red ....You wish yourself dead.

Black ....You will wish yourself back.

Gray ....You shall travel far away.

Pink ....Of you he'll always think.

Green ....You are ashamed to be seen.

FLOWERS AND THEIR MEANINGS

Acacia, yellow	Secret love
Bachelor's Button	Celibacy
Cranberry	Cure for heartache
Daffodil	Regard
Everlasting Pea	Lasting pleasure
Forget-me-not	True love
Geranium, Ivy	Bridal favor
Honeysuckle	Devoted affection
Indian Jasmine (Ipomoea)	Attachment
Juniper	Protection
Kennedia	Mental beauty
Lotus Flower	Estranged love
Motherwort	Concealed love
Nightshade	Truth
Orange Blossoms	Your purity equals loveliness
Peach Blossoms	I am your captive
Queen's Rocket	Queen of coquettes
Quince	Temptation
Rose	Love
Sweet William	Gallantry
Tuberose	Dangerous pleasure
Veronica	Fidelity
Water Lily	Purity of heart
Xeranthemum	Cheerfulness in adversity
Yew	Sorrow
Zinnia	Thoughts of absent friends

LA BOHÈME

MUSIC BY GIACOMO PUCCINI (1858–1924)

ACT I

It's Christmas Eve in the Latin Quarter of Paris in about 1830. In their cold attic room, the painter Marcello and poet Rodolfo are trying to keep warm by burning pages from Rodolfo's latest play. They're joined by their friends—first Colline, a young philosopher, and then Schaunard, a musician who has been playing his violin for money and has brought fuel and wine. They are interrupted by an unexpected visit from their land-lord, Benoit, who's come to collect the rent. They ply the older man with wine, until he tells them of his sexual indiscretions, at which point they chuck him out in feigned shock. As the friends leave for a meal at the nearby Café Momus, Rodolfo promises to join them soon, staying behind to finish writing an article. There is a knock at the door: a neighbor, Mimi, says her candle has gone out on the drafty stairs. Mimi feels faint and Rodolfo offers her some wine. He also relights her candle and helps her to the door. Mimi realizes she's lost her key and as the two search for it, both candles are blown out. In the moon-light the poet takes the girl's freezing cold hand and tells her about his life and his dreams.

"Che Gelida Manina"	*"Your little hand is frozen"*
ITALIAN	ENGLISH
RODOLFO.	RODOLFO.
Che gelida manina	Your little hand is frozen,
se la lasci riscaldar	Let me warm it for you.

Cercar che giova?	There's no point in looking for the key.
Al buio non si trova.	We won't find it in the dark.
Ma per fortuna	But we're lucky,
é una notte di luna,	The moon is out tonight,
e qui la luna	And the moon
l'abbiamo vicina.	Is near and dear to us.
Aspetti, signorina,	So wait a moment, young lady,
le dirò con due parole	While I tell you in just a couple of words
chi son,	Who I am,
chi son,	What I do,
e che faccio,	And how I earn my living.
come vivo. Vuole?	Would you like that?
Chi son? Sono un poeta.	Who am I? I am a poet.
Che cosa faccio? Scrivo.	What do I do? I write.
E come vivo? Vivo!	And how do I make a living? I just live.
In povertà mia lieta	I am very poor but very happy,
scialo da gran signore	as if I were a wealthy gentleman,
rime ed inni d'amore.	I squander my rhymes and hymns of love.
Per sogni e per chimere	For my dreams and illusions
e per castelli in aria,	And castles in the air have
l'anima ho milionaria.	made me a millionaire.

Talor dal mio forziere

ruban tutti i gioelli due ladri,
    gli occhi belli.

V'entrar con voi pur ora,

ed i miei sogni usati

e i bei sogni miei,

tosto si dileguar!

Ma il furto non m'accora,

poiché, poiché v'ha preso
    stanza

la speranza!

Or che mi conoscete,

parlate voi, deh! Parlate.

Chi siete?

Vi piaccia dir!

Sometimes two thieves,

Steal the jewels out of my
    safe, beautiful eyes.

They came in with you just
    now

And my worn-out dreams,

My once lovely dreams,

Immediately vanished.

But the robbery doesn't
    bother me,

Because, well because

The hope of love has taken
    their place.

Now that you know all about
    me,

Tell me about yourself.

Speak to me! Who are you?

I really want to know.

YOUR LOVE LIFE, ACCORDING TO YOUR PALM

The love line is the top line on your palm, starting at the edge on the pinkie side and ending at the base of the index finger.

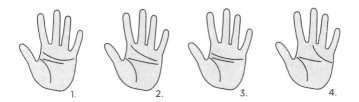

1. A curved love line means you are sensitive.
2. A line that ends between the index and middle fingers means you are passionate and emotional.
3. A line that goes straight across means you are intellectual, more of a thinker than a lover.
4. A line that ends just under the base of the middle finger means you are selfish in love.

BRIGHT STAR!

JOHN KEATS (1795-1821)

Bright star, would I were steadfast as thou art—
Not in lone splendour hung aloft the night,
And watching, with eternal lids apart,
Like Nature's patient sleepless Eremite,
The moving waters at their priestlike task
Of pure ablution round earth's human shores,
Or gazing on the new soft fallen mask
Of snow upon the mountains and the moors—
No—yet still steadfast, still unchangeable,
Pillow'd upon my fair love's ripening breast,
To feel for ever its soft fall and swell,
Awake for ever in a sweet unrest,
Still, still to hear her tender-taken breath,
And so live ever—or else swoon to death.

WHAT MAKES WOMEN
FEEL BEAUTIFUL

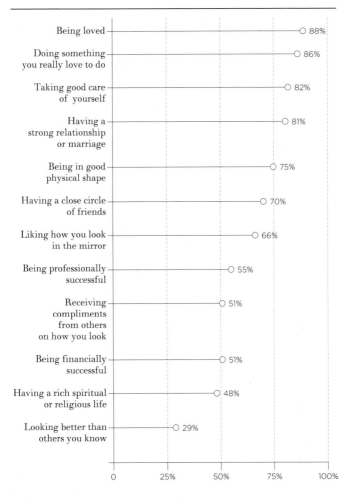

Being loved	88%
Doing something you really love to do	86%
Taking good care of yourself	82%
Having a strong relationship or marriage	81%
Being in good physical shape	75%
Having a close circle of friends	70%
Liking how you look in the mirror	66%
Being professionally successful	55%
Receiving compliments from others on how you look	51%
Being financially successful	51%
Having a rich spiritual or religious life	48%
Looking better than others you know	29%

0   25%   50%   75%   100%

TONGUE

ZBIGNIEW HERBERT (1924–98)

Inadvertently I passed the border of her teeth and swallowed her agile tongue. It lives inside me now, like a Japanese fish. It brushes against my heart and my diaphragm as if against the walls of an aquarium. It stirs silt from the bottom.

She whom I deprived of a voice stares at me with big eyes and waits for a word.

Yet I do not know which tongue to use when speaking to her—the stolen one or the one which melts in my mouth from an excess of heavy goodness.

RATIO OF MEN TO WOMEN
FOR THIRTEEN GENERATIONS (U. S.)

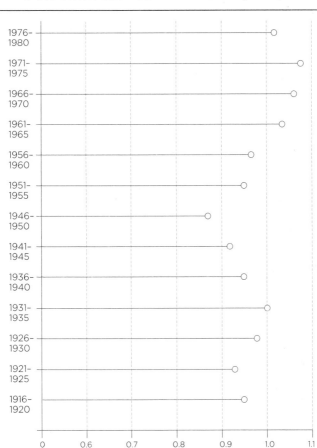

CLASSIC TV COUPLES

COUPLE	TV SHOW
Lucy & Ricky	*I Love Lucy*
Ward & June	*Leave It to Beaver*
Ozzie & Harriet	*The Adventures of Ozzie and Harriet*
Mike & Carol	*The Brady Bunch*
Gomez & Morticia	*The Addams Family*
Heathcliff & Clair	*The Cosby Show*
Rob & Laura	*The Dick Van Dyke Show*
Ralph & Alice	*The Honeymooners*
Thurston & Lovey	*Gilligan's Island*
Archie & Edith	*All in the Family*
Wilma & Fred	*The Flintstones*
Sam & Diane	*Cheers*
Carrie & Mr. Big (John)	*Sex and the City*
Homer & Marge	*The Simpsons*
Fred & Daphne	*Scooby-Doo, Where Are You?*
Frisco & Felicia	*General Hospital*
Jonathan & Jennifer	*Hart to Hart*
David & Maddie	*Moonlighting*

EFFECTS OF LOVE ON HORMONES

Hormonal levels of subjects in the early stage of falling in love compared to those of control subjects.

	SUBJECTS IN LOVE		CONTROL SUBJECTS	
	M	F	M	F
FSH	3.2 ± 1.1	8.1 ± 4.2	9.3 ± 3.8	9.1 ± 3.1
LH	6.9 ± 2.3	12.3 ± 3.4	7.1 ± 2.8	10 ± 4.3
Estradiol	< 50	170 ± 23	< 50	145 ± 32
Progesterone	< 0.2	0.57 ± 0.3	< 0.2	0.55 ± 0.3
Testosterone	4.1 ± 1.0	1.2 ± 0.4	6.8 ± 2.1	0.6 ± 0.2
DHEAS	2736 ± 1122	2232 ± 986	2450 ± 1000	2315 ± 980
Cortisol	224 ± 21	243 ± 41	165 ± 21	172 ± 44
Androstene-dione	2.0 ± 1.0	2.1 ± 0.7	2.1 ± 0.7	1.9 ± 0.7

= statistically significant

All measurements in ng/ml.

Subjects were required to have begun a love relationship within the previous six months (mean+SD: 3±1 months) and at least four hours a day had to have been spent in thinking about the partner (mean+SD: 9±3 hours), as recorded by a specifically designed questionnaire.

Twenty-four subjects (twelve female and twelve male, mean age±SD: 29±3), with either a long-lasting or no relationship, served as the control group.

SONNET 18

WILLIAM SHAKESPEARE (1564–1616)

Shall I compare thee to a summer's day?
Thou art more lovely and more temperate:
Rough winds do shake the darling buds of May,
And summer's lease hath all too short a date:
Sometime too hot the eye of heaven shines,
And often is his gold complexion dimm'd;
And every fair from fair sometime declines,
By chance or nature's changing course untrimm'd;
But thy eternal summer shall not fade
Nor lose possession of that fair thou owest;
Nor shall Death brag thou wander'st in his shade,
When in eternal lines to time thou growest:
So long as men can breathe or eyes can see,
So long lives this and this gives life to thee.

GODS AND GODDESSES OF LOVE

NAME	ORIGIN	DESCRIPTION
Juno	Roman	Goddess of heaven and the moon; the protector of women, particularly those in labor (wife of Jupiter)
Venus	Roman	Goddess of love and desire
Cupid (AKA *Amor*)	Roman	God of love, passion, and desire (Venus's son)
Branwen	Celtic	Goddess of love, sexuality, and the sea
Freya	Norse	Goddess of love, beauty, fertility, and war
Inanna	Sumerian	Goddess of love, fertility, and war
Ani-Ibo	African	Goddess of birth, death, happiness, and love
Hathor	Egyptian	Goddess of love, music, and beauty
Kamadeva	Indian	God of love (son of Lakshmi and Vishnu)
Lakshmi	Indian (Hindu)	Goddess of love and beauty
Vishnu	Indian (Hindu)	God of love
Aizen-Myo-o	Japanese (Buddhist)	God of love and beauty

B&D	=	Bondage & Discipline	GBF =	Gay Black Female
BBW	=	Big Beautiful Woman	GBM =	Gay Black Male
BDSM=		Any subset of B&D,	GWF =	Gay White Female
		D/S, and SM	GWM =	Gay White Male
BHM	=	Big Handsome Man	HWP =	Height and Weight
BiF	=	Bisexual Female		Proportional
BiM	=	Bisexual Male	ICQ =	I Seek You
BiMF	=	Bisexual Married	IRC =	Internet Relay Chat
		Female	IRL =	In Real Life
BiMM	=	Bisexual Married	ISO =	In Search Of
		Male	LDR =	Long Distance
CD	=	Cross-dresser		Relationship
CPL	=	Couple	LTR =	Long Term
DBF	=	Divorced Black		Relationship
		Female	MBA =	Married but Available
DBM	=	Divorced Black Male	MBF =	Married Black Female
DDF	=	Drug and Disease	MBM =	Married Black Male
		Free	MJF =	Married Jewish
Dom	=	Dominant		Female
D/S	=	Domination/	MJM =	Married Jewish Male
		Submission	MM =	Married Men
DWF	=	Divorced White	MWC =	Married with Children
		Female	MtF =	Male to Female
DWM	=	Divorced White Male		Transgendered
F/T	=	Full Time	MWF =	Married White
FtM	=	Female to Male		Female
		Transgendered	MWM =	Married White Male

N/S	= Non-Smoker		SITCOM	= Single Income Two Children Oppressive Mortgage
PF	= Professional Female			
PM	= Professional Male			
P/T	= Part Time		SJF	= Single Jewish Female
RL	= Real Life		SJM	= Single Jewish Male
SAF	= Single Asian Female		SM	= Sadism/Masochism
SALT	= Single and Loving It		SOH	= Sense of Humor
SAM	= Single Asian Male		SPARK	= Single Parent Raising Kids
SBF	= Single Black Female			
SBM	= Single Black Male		Sub	= Submissive
SCF	= Single Christian Female		SWF	= Single White Female
			SWM	= Single White Male
SCM	= Single Christian Male		TDY	= Temporarily Divorced Yesterday
SHF	= Single Hispanic Female			
			TG	= Transgender
SHM	= Single Hispanic Male		TS	= Transsexual
SINK	= Single Income No Kids		TV	= Transvestite
			W/E	= Well-Endowed

93% of romance readers are women.

49.5% of romance readers are married.

33.3% of romance readers are single.

10.7% of romance readers are divorced.

6% of romance readers are widowed.

1% of romance readers are under the age of 14.

3% of romance readers are between the ages of 14 and 16.

4% of romance readers are between the ages of 17 and 19.

8% of romance readers are between the ages of 20 and 24.

21% of romance readers are between the ages of 25 and 34.

25% of romance readers are between the ages of 35 and 44.

17% of romance readers are between the ages of 45 and 54.

10% of romance readers are between the ages of 55 and 64.

8% of romance readers are between the ages of 65 and 74.

3% of romance readers are 75 or older.

71% of romance readers say they read their first romance at
age 16 or younger.

5% of romance readers have some high-school education
or less.

32% of romance readers are high-school graduates.

22% of romance readers have attended vocational school
or some college.

21% of romance readers are college graduates.

10% of romance readers have attended post-graduate
programs.

75% of romance readers are white.

11% of romance readers are African American.

11% of romance readers are Hispanic.

57% of romance readers read between 1 and 5 romances each year.

17% of romance readers read between 6 and 10 romances each year.

8% of romance readers read between 11 and 20 romances per year.

12% of romance readers read between 21 and 50 romances per year.

4% of romance readers read between 51 and 100 romances per year.

2% of romance readers read more than 100 romances per year.

Romance novels generated $1.41 billion in sales in 2003.

2,093 romance titles were released in 2003.

Romance fiction comprises 18% of all books sold (not including children's books).

32% of the reading population in the Midwest reads romance fiction.

26% of the reading population in the West reads romance fiction.

20% of the reading population in the South reads romance fiction.

16% of the reading population in the Northeast reads romance fiction.

COMPANY	DESCRIPTION	COST	
Americansingles americansingles.com	"Find a date, a friend, or more!"	$24.95/month $59.95/3 months	$99.95/6 months $199.95/1 year
eHarmony eharmony.com	"The fastest growing relation-ship site on the Web."	$49.95/month $99.95/3 months	$159.95/6 months $249.95/1 year
Jdate jdate.com	"The largest Jewish singles network."	$34.95/month $99.95/3 months $149.00/6 months	
AOL personals love.com	"Search to your heart's content."	$14.94/month $39.95/3 months	$59.95/6 months $79.95/1 year
Match match.com	The world's biggest online dating service, with 15 million members.	$29.99/month $50.97/3 months $77.94/6 months	
Matchmaker matchmaker.com	"By the time you meet, you know."	$44.95/3 months $74.95/6 months $99.95/1 year	
The Millionaire's Club millionairesclub123.com	"Where successful men go to find their beautiful and intelligent wives."	Free for women $10,000/year for "Gold Membership" $20,000/year for "Platinum Membership"	
Yahoo! personals yahoo.com	"Better first dates, more second dates!"	$19.95/1 month $44.95/3 months $99.95/1 year	

*American singles spent a total of $214.3 million dollars on online personals in the first half of 2003.

MEDIAN AGE OF FIRST MARRIAGE (U.S.)

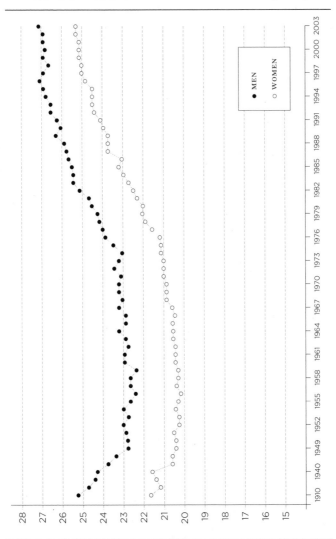

THE GOOD-MORROW

JOHN DONNE (1572–1631)

I wonder, by my troth, what thou and I
Did, till we loved? were we not weaned till then?
But sucked on country pleasures, childishly?
Or snorted we in the Seven Sleepers' den?
'Twas so; but this, all pleasures fancies be.
If ever any beauty I did see,
Which I desired, and got, 'twas but a dream of thee.

And now good-morrow to our waking souls,
Which watch not one another out of fear;
For love all love of other sights controls,
And makes one little room an everywhere.
Let sea-discoverers to new worlds have gone
Let maps to others, worlds on worlds have shown,
Let us possess one world, each hath one, and is one.

My face in thine eye, thine in mine appears,
And true plain hearts do in the faces rest;
Where can we find two better hemispheres,
Without sharp north, without declining west?
Whatever dies, was not mixed equally;
If our two loves be one, or thou and I
Love so alike that none can slacken, none can die.

OXYTOCIN, THE LOVE HORMONE
$C_{43}H_{66}N_{12}O_{12}S_2$

Oxytocin is a neuropeptide thought to induce pair bonding.
Its levels are found to be highest in people falling in love.

The hormone also stimulates uterine contractions, lactation,
and maternal behavior, as well as playing a role in male and
female orgasms.

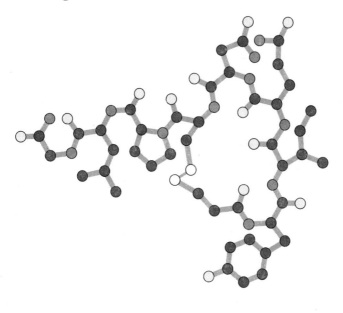

SAMPLE PRENUPTIAL AGREEMENT

Be it known, this agreement is entered into on the
_____ day of _____, 20___ between
_____ and _____

Whereas, the parties contemplate legal marriage under
the laws of the State of _____, and it is their
mutual desire to enter into this agreement so that they
will continue to own and control their own property, and
are getting married because of their love for each other
but do not desire that their present respective financial
interests be changed by their marriage. Now, therefore, it
is agreed as follows:

1. All property that belongs to each of the above parties
shall be, and shall forever remain, their personal estate,
including all interest, rents, and profits that may accrue
from said property, and said property shall remain forever
free of claim by the other.

2. The parties shall have at all times the full right and
authority, in all respects the same as each would have if
not married, to use, sell, enjoy, manage, gift and convey
all property that may presently belong to him or her.

3. In the event of a separation or divorce, the parties shall
have no right against each other by way of claims for support, alimony, maintenance, compensation, or division of
property existing of this date.

4. In the event of separation or divorce, marital property acquired after marriage shall nevertheless remain subject to division, either by agreement or judicial determination.

5. This agreement shall be binding and inure to the benefit of the parties, their successors, assigns, and personal representatives.

This agreement shall be enforced with the laws of the State of _____.

Signed this _____ day of _____, 20__

Witnessed:

_____

_____
Witness First Party

_____

_____
Witness Second Party

TO HIS COY MISTRESS

ANDREW MARVELL (1621–78)

Had we but world enough, and time,
This coyness, lady, were no crime.
We would sit down and think which way
To walk, and pass our long love's day;
Thou by the Indian Ganges' side
Shouldst rubies find; I by the tide
Of Humber would complain. I would
Love you ten years before the Flood;
And you should, if you please, refuse
Till the conversion of the Jews.
My vegetable love should grow
Vaster than empires, and more slow.
An hundred years should go to praise
Thine eyes, and on thy forehead gaze;
Two hundred to adore each breast,
But thirty thousand to the rest;
An age at least to every part,
And the last age should show your heart.
For, lady, you deserve this state,
Nor would I love at lower rate.

But at my back I always hear
Time's winged chariot hurrying near;
And yonder all before us lie
Deserts of vast eternity.
Thy beauty shall no more be found,

Nor, in thy marble vault, shall sound
My echoing song; then worms shall try
That long preserv'd virginity,
And your quaint honour turn to dust,
And into ashes all my lust.
The grave's a fine and private place,
But none I think do there embrace.

Now therefore, while the youthful hue
Sits on thy skin like morning dew,
And while thy willing soul transpires
At every pore with instant fires,
Now let us sport us while we may;
And now, like am'rous birds of prey,
Rather at once our time devour,
Than languish in his slow-chapp'd power.
Let us roll all our strength, and all
Our sweetness, up into one ball;
And tear our pleasures with rough strife
Thorough the iron gates of life.
Thus, though we cannot make our sun
Stand still, yet we will make him run.

COMMON DREAM SYMBOLS
AND THEIR MEANINGS

Baby: A love affair may be blooming for you in the near future.

Balloon: To dream of a balloon indicates a dashing of hope on any and all fronts, business or love.

Bed: If a woman dreams of making a bed, there will soon be a new lover in her life.

Birth: For unmarried women, a birth dream indicates inevitable unchastity. For married women, it indicates happy confinement.

Bride, bridegroom: To dream of a bride or bridegroom indicates sorrow and disappointment.

Cats: To dream of cats signifies treachery as well as a run of bad luck.

Corpse: To dream of a corpse indicates a hasty and imprudent engagement in which you will be unhappy.

Garden: To see a flower garden foretells of tranquility, comfort, true love, and happy home in your future.

Gloves: To find a pair of gloves in a dream denotes a marriage or new love affair.

Honey: To dream of eating honey foretells that you will attain wealth and love.

Husband: If you dream about falling in love with another woman's husband, it indicates that you are growing vicious.

Jail: To dream that your lover is in jail signifies that the lover is deceitful and untrustworthy.

Limbs: Breakage of limbs in a dream indicates breakage of a marriage vow.

Marriage: A marriage in a dream is a sign of a death in the family. If the marriage is between strangers, then the death pertains to a not-too-close acquaintance or friend.

Necklace: If you dream your loved one places a necklace around your neck or that you are wearing one, it shows an early marriage and a happy domestic life.

Nectar: To drink nectar in dream indicates riches and prosperity. You will marry a handsome person in high life and live in great state.

Oak tree: If a newlywed sees many oak trees in a forest it foretells a long marriage and many children.

River: A dream of rapid and flowing muddy river indicates great troubles and difficulties. But a river with calm glassy surface foretells happiness and love.

Rose: A rose received in a dream in springtime means you will find true love; received in winter, your search will be fruitless.

Running: Running is a sign of a big change in your life.

Snakes: To dream of many snakes in a pit means bad luck in love or business.

Spiders: All spiders except tarantulas are omens of good luck. The larger the spider, the bigger the rewards.

Teeth: If you dream your teeth are rotten, crooked, or falling out, your lies are hurting someone very badly and you will soon be found out.

Yarn: To dream of yarn signifies you will soon become the wife of a wealthy man.

MATE POACHING IN THE 21ST CENTURY
OCCURANCE AND SUCCESS OF STEALING A MATE ACROSS TEN WORLD REGIONS

	Have you ever attempted to poach for short-term mating?		Have you ever attempted to poach for long-term mating?	
WORLD REGIONS	MEN%	WOMEN%	MEN%	WOMEN%
North America	62.1	39.9	63.4	51.5
South America	70.3	38.2	65.6	50.2
Western Europe	56.7	39.2	56.2	46.0
Eastern Europe	66.6	41.9	59.9	43.3
Southern Europe	64.3	35.5	60.0	44.0
Middle East	52.0	27.1	53.5	38.9
Africa	56.7	22.9	63.4	28.7
Oceania	61.0	42.2	49.8	42.3
South/ Southeast Asia	51.4	26.6	38.9	17.4
East Asia	29.5	14.9	47.4	33.5
	Did you poach your current partner in your relationship?		Did your current partner poach you in your relationship?	
WORLD REGIONS	MEN%	WOMEN%	MEN%	WOMEN%
North America	10.4	7.7	10.8	13.6
South America	8.2	6.8	7.9	9.9
Western Europe	9.4	7.9	5.9	10.7
Eastern Europe	17.8	11.7	11.2	20.0
Southern Europe	10.3	7.6	11.0	12.6
Middle East	8.6	6.0	6.8	10.0
Africa	17.3	10.7	17.7	18.0
Oceania	3.4	6.6	4.0	9.9
South/ Southeast Asia	17.3	11.1	12.1	15.9
East Asia	7.6	5.8	7.2	12.4

RIGHT ROYAL WEDDINGS

November 6, 1935	Princess Alice & the Duke of Gloucester	Buckingham Palace
November 20, 1947	Queen Elizabeth & Prince Phillip	Westminster Abbey
May 6, 1960	Princess Margaret & Antony Armstrong-Jones	Westminster Abbey
June 8, 1961	The Duke of Kent & Katharine Worsley	York Minster
April 24, 1963	Princess Alexandra & Angus Ogilvy	Westminster Abbey
July 8, 1972	Prince Richard & Birgitte Eva van Deurs	St Andrews Church, Barnwell, Northamptonshire
November 14, 1973	Princess Anne & Mark Phillips	Westminster Abbey (Divorced 1992)
June 30, 1978	Prince Michael of Kent & Baroness Marie-Christine von Reibnitz	Vienna
July 29, 1981	Prince Charles & Diana Spencer	St Paul's Cathedral (Divorced 1996)
July 23, 1986	Prince Andrew & Sarah Ferguson	Westminster Abbey (Divorced 1996)
December 12, 1992	Princess Anne & Timothy Lawrence	Crathie Church, Scotland
June 19, 1999	Prince Edward & Sophie Rhys-Jones	St. Georges Chapel, Windsor
April 9, 2005	Prince Charles & Camilla Parker-Bowles	Windsor Guildhall, Berkshire

"A Deep-Sworn Vow"

Others because you did not keep
That deep-sworn vow have been friends of mine;
But always when I look death in the face,
When I clamber to the heights of sleep,
Or when I grow excited with wine,
Suddenly I meet your face.

"Memory"

One had a lovely face,
And two or three had charm,
But charm and face were in vain
Because the mountain grass
Cannot but keep the form
Where the mountain hare has lain.

VALENTINE'S DAY ECONOMICS

The amount the average American man spends on
Valentine's Day: $125

The amount the average American woman spends on
Valentine's Day: $38

Percent of Americans give their beloved a Valentine
card: >80%

Estimated number of roses grown for Valentine's Day 2004:
175 million.

Percentage of flowers bought by men: 66%

Percentage of flowers bought by women: 34%

In AD 270, the Roman emperor Claudius II decided that single men made better soldiers and so he banned marriage for young men. A priest named Valentine began marrying Roman lovers in secret. When Claudius found out, he threw Valentine in prison.

In prison, Valentine fell in love with a young blind girl, his jailer's daughter. His love was so strong that he succeeded in restoring the girl's sight. Just before he died, he wrote her a letter, signing it "From your Valentine." He was put to death in February of that year.

The month of his death was already associated with romance and love. In mid-February, a celebration honoring the god Lupercus took place to commemorate young men's rites of passage. During this celebration, young men would draw names of young women from a lottery box. The young woman whose name was drawn would become her man's sexual partner for the rest of the year. In an effort to steer the festival away from the pagan god Lupercus, the Church searched for a patron saint of love. The martyred Valentine seemed a fitting alternative; thus for hundreds of years lovers have declared their devotion to each other with Valentine's messages on February 14.

MARITAL STATUS OF THE POPULATION
15 YEARS OLD AND OVER (U.S.)

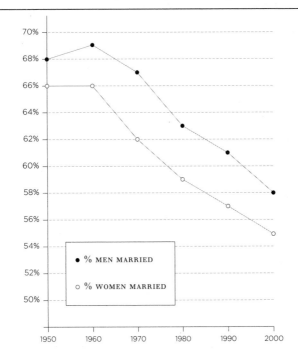

Afrikaans (South Africa)	*Ek het jou lief*
Albanian	*Une te dua*
Arabic	*nhebuk*
Bulgarian	*Obicham te*
Burmese	*Nin ko nga chitde; Chit pa de*
Catalan	*T'estimo*
Chinese	*Ngo oi ney* (Canton)
Croatian	*Volim te*
Czech	*Miluji té*
Danish	*Jeg elsker dig*
Dutch	*Ik hou van jou*
Esperanto	*Mi amas vin*
Finnish	*Minä rakastan sinua*
French	*Je t'aime*
German	*Ich liebe dich*
Greek	*S'ayapo*
Hawaiian	*Aloha au ia 'oe*
Hebrew	*Ani ohev otach* (M TO F)
	Ani ohev otcha (F TO M)
Hindi	*Mai tumase pyar karata hun* (M TO F)
	Mai tumase pyar karati hun (F TO M)
Hungarian	*Szeretlek*
Icelandic	*Ég elska thig*
Irish	*Taim i'ngra leat*
Italian	*Ti amo*
Japanese	*Aishite imasu*
Korean	*Tangsinul sarang hayo*

Latin	*Te amo*
Norwegian	*Eg elskar deg*
Polish	*Kocham Cie*
Portuguese	*Eu te amo*
Rumanian	*Te iubesc*
Russian	*Ya tebya lyublyu*
Serbian; Serbo-Croatian	*Ljubim te; Volim te;*
Sioux	*Techihhila*
Spanish	*Te amo*
Swahili	*Nakupenda Wewe*
Swedish	*Jag älskar dig*
Tagalog	*Mahal kita*
Thai	*Phom Rak Khun* (M TO F)
	Ch'an Rak Khun (F TO M)
Tunisian	*Ha eh bak*
Turkish	*Seni seviyorum*
Urdu	*Me aap se pyaar karthi houn*
Vietnamese	*Toi yeu em*
Welsh	*Rwy'n dy garu di*
Zulu	*Ngiyakuthanda*

"I LOVE YOU" IN SIGN LANGUAGE

"I": Point at self with index finger.

"Love": Hold crossed hands over chest.

"You": Point with index finger to the other person.

Or:

TRADITIONAL
WEDDING ANNIVERSARY GIFTS

FIRST	Paper
SECOND	Cotton
THIRD	Leather
FOURTH	Fruit/Flowers
FIFTH	Wood
SIXTH	Iron/Sweets
SEVENTH	Wool/Copper
EIGHTH	Bronze/Pottery
NINTH	Pottery/China/Willow
TENTH	Tin/Aluminum
ELEVENTH	Steel
TWELFTH	Silk/Linen
THIRTEENTH	Lace
FOURTEENTH	Ivory
FIFTEENTH	Crystal
TWENTIETH	China, Porcelain
TWENTY-FIFTH	Silver
THIRTIETH	Pearl
THIRTY-FIFTH	Coral
FORTIETH	Ruby
FORTY-FIFTH	Sapphire
FIFTIETH	Gold
FIFTY-FIFTH	Emerald
SIXTIETH	Diamond

SONNETS FROM THE PORTUGUESE XLIII
ELIZABETH BARRETT BROWNING (1806–61)

How do I love thee? Let me count the ways.
I love thee to the depth and breadth and height
My soul can reach, when feeling out of sight
For the ends of Being and ideal Grace.
I love thee to the level of everyday's
Most quiet need, by sun and candle-light.
I love thee freely, as men strive for Right;
I love thee purely, as they turn from Praise.
I love thee with a passion put to use
In my old griefs, and with my childhood's faith.
I love thee with a love I seemed to lose
With my lost saints,—I love thee with the breath,
Smiles, tears, of all my life!—and, if God choose,
I shall but love thee better after death.

LEGAL AGE OF CONSENT
AROUND THE WORLD*

COUNTRY	M/F SEX	M/M SEX	F/F SEX
Algeria	16	Illegal	Illegal
Antigua (Barbuda)	16	18	16
Armenia	16	Illegal	Illegal
Australia	16	16	16
Austria	14	18	14
Bahamas	16	18	18
Bermuda	16	18	16
Canada	14	14/18	14
Chile	12	18	18
China	14	Not defined	Not defined
China: Hong Kong	16	21	?
Colombia	12/14	14	14
Costa Rica	15/16	15/Illegal	15/Illegal
Croatia	14	14/18	14/18
Cuba	16	16	16
Czech Republic	15	15	15
Denmark	15	15	15
Eritrea	18	18	18
Estonia	14	16	16
Islas Malvinas	16	18	16
Faroe Island	15	18	18
Finland	16	16	16
France	15	15	15
Germany	14/16	14/16	14/16
Greece	15/17	17	15/17
Grenada	17	Illegal	Illegal
Guadeloupe	15	15	15
Guatemala	18	18	18
Guyana	13	Illegal	Illegal
Haiti	18	18	18
Honduras	14/17	14	14
Hungary	14	14	14
Iceland	14	14	14
India	16	Illegal	Illegal
Indonesia	17	Not defined	Not defined
Iran	17/14	Illegal	Illegal
Ireland	17	17	17
Israel	16	16	16

COUNTRY	M/F SEX	M/M SEX	F/F SEX
Italy	14	14	14
Jamaica	16	Illegal	Illegal
Japan	13	13	13
Jordan	16	Illegal	Illegal
Kenya	16	Illegal	Illegal
Korea	13	13	13
Kosovo	14	18	14
Lebanon	15/18	Illegal	Illegal
Liberia	16	Unknown	Unknown
Liechtenstein	14	14/18	14
Lithuania	16	18	16
Luxembourg	16	16	16
Madagascar	21	21	21
Mali	16	Unknown	Unknown
Malta	12/18	12/18	12/18
Martinique	15	15	15
Mauritius	15	Illegal	Illegal
México	12	18	18
Moldova	16	16	16
Monaco	15	15	15
Montenegro	14	14	14
Morocco	15	Unknown	Unknown
Namibia	16	Unknown	Unknown
Nepal	16	Unknown	Unknown
Netherlands	12/16	12/16	12/16
Netherlands Antilles	16	16	16
New Caledonia	15	15	15
New Zealand	16	16	16
Norway	16	16	16
Oman	Not defined	Illegal	Illegal
Papua New Guinea	16	Illegal	16
Peru	14	14	14
Poland	15	15	15
Puerto Rico	14	Illegal	Illegal
Romania	14	Illegal	Illegal
Rwanda	18	18	18
San Marino	14/16	14/16	14/16
Saudi Arabia	Must be married	Illegal	Illegal

THEORIES ON THE ORIGINS OF
LEAP YEAR PROPOSALS

The leap year tradition of women proposing to men may have begun in fifth-century Ireland. St. Bridget complained to St. Patrick about how long women had to wait for a proposal from a man. So St. Patrick decided that impatient ladies could propose on February 29.

Alternately, the leap year tradition of women proposing to men may be linked to a loophole in English law. Hundreds of years ago, the date of February 29 was not recognized by the law, and thus had no legal status. Furthermore, the day only existed to correct a discrepancy in the calendar year and thus could also be used to correct the age-old discrepancy over who was allowed to propose to whom.

In writing, the leap year tradition of women proposing to men dates back to 1288. That year, Scottish law first permitted a woman to propose marriage to a man. A second law imposed a fine on any man who declined the proposal.

TOP 100 MOST PASSIONATE FILMS OF ALL TIME, ACCORDING TO THE AMERICAN FILM INSTITUTE

1. *Casablanca* (1942)
2. *Gone with the Wind* (1939)
3. *West Side Story* (1961)
4. *Roman Holiday* (1953)
5. *An Affair to Remember* (1957)
6. *The Way We Were* (1973)
7. *Doctor Zhivago* (1965)
8. *It's a Wonderful Life* (1946)
9. *Love Story* (1970)
10. *City Lights* (1931)
11. *Annie Hall* (1977)
12. *My Fair Lady* (1964)
13. *Out of Africa* (1985)
14. *The African Queen* (1951)
15. *Wuthering Heights* (1939)
16. *Singin' in the Rain* (1952)
17. *Moonstruck* (1987)
18. *Vertigo* (1958)
19. *Ghost* (1990)
20. *From Here to Eternity* (1953)
21. *Pretty Woman* (1990)
22. *On Golden Pond* (1981)
23. *Now, Voyager* (1942)
24. *King Kong* (1933)
25. *When Harry Met Sally . . .* (1989)
26. *The Lady Eve* (1941)
27. *The Sound of Music* (1965)
28. *The Shop Around the Corner* (1940)
29. *An Officer and A Gentleman* (1982)
30. *Swing Time* (1936)
31. *The King and I* (1956)
32. *Dark Victory* (1939)
33. *Camille* (1937)
34. *Beauty and the Beast* (1991)
35. *Gigi* (1958)
36. *Random Harvest* (1942)
37. *Titanic* (1997)

38. *It Happened One Night* (1934)

39. *An American in Paris* (1951)

40. *Ninotchka* (1939)

41. *Funny Girl* (1968)

42. *Anna Karenina* (1935)

43. *A Star Is Born* (1954)

44. *The Philadelphia Story* (1940)

45. *Sleepless in Seattle* (1993)

46. *To Catch a Thief* (1955)

47. *Splendor in the Grass* (1961)

48. *Last Tango in Paris* (1972)

49. *The Postman Always Rings Twice* (1946)

50. *Shakespeare in Love* (1998)

51. *Bringing Up Baby* (1938)

52. *The Graduate* (1967)

53. *A Place in the Sun* (1951)

54. *Sabrina* (1954)

55. *Reds* (1981)

56. *The English Patient* (1996)

57. *Two for the Road* (1967)

58. *Guess Who's Coming to Dinner* (1967)

59. *Picnic* (1955)

60. *To Have and Have Not* (1944)

61. *Breakfast at Tiffany's* (1961)

62. *The Apartment* (1960)

63. *Sunrise* (1927)

64. *Marty* (1955)

65. *Bonnie and Clyde* (1967)

66. *Manhattan* (1979)

67. *A Streetcar Named Desire* (1951)

68. *What's Up, Doc?* (1972)

69. *Harold and Maude* (1971)

70. *Sense and Sensibility* (1995)

71. *Way Down East* (1920)

72. *Roxanne* (1987)

73. *The Ghost and Mrs. Muir* (1947)

74. *Woman of the Year* (1942)
75. *The American President* (1995)
76. *The Quiet Man* (1952)
77. *The Awful Truth* (1937)
78. *Coming Home* (1978)
79. *Jezebel* (1939)
80. *The Sheik* (1921)
81. *The Goodbye Girl* (1977)
82. *Witness* (1985)
83. *Morocco* (1930)
84. *Double Indemnity* (1944)
85. *Love Is a Many-Splendored Thing* (1955)
86. *Notorious* (1946)
87. *The Unbearable Lightness of Being* (1988)
88. *The Princess Bride* (1987)
89. *Who's Afraid of Virginia Woolf?* (1966)
90. *The Bridges of Madison County* (1991)
91. *Working Girl* (1988)
92. *Porgy and Bess* (1959)
93. *Dirty Dancing* (1987)
94. *Body Heat* (1981)
95. *Lady and the Tramp* (1955)
96. *Barefoot in the Park* (1967)
97. *Grease* (1978)
98. *The Hunchback of Notre Dame* (1939)
99. *Pillow Talk* (1959)
100. *Jerry Maguire* (1996)

PROVERBS ON LOVE AND MARRIAGE

Absence makes the heart grow fonder.

Beauty is in the eye of the beholder.

Wedlock is a padlock.

Love begets love.

Lucky at cards, unlucky in love.

Love is blind.

Marry in haste, repent at leisure.

One cannot love and be wise.

Needles and pins, needles and pins,
when a man marries his troubles begin.

Cold hands, warm heart.

A young man married is a young man marred.

Love laughs at locksmiths.

Please your eye and plague your heart.

Never marry for money, but marry where money is.

There's more to marriage than four bare legs in a bed.

Love and a cough cannot be hid.

All's fair in love and war.

It's better to have loved and lost,
than never to have loved at all.

ASPARAGUS: Rich in vitamin E, is thought to stimulate sex hormones.

BASIL: Used in voodoo love ceremonies in Haiti as an offering to Erzulie, the voodoo love goddess.

CHILI PEPPER: The pepper's heat is generated by capsaicin, a chemical that stimulates nerve-endings. Also, raises the pulse.

DAMIANA: Also called wild yam, formerly used for medicinal purposes by indigenous peoples of Central America. Now associated with helping erectile dysfunctions, although with no scientific proof.

EGGS: A symbol of fertility.

FIGS: Soft and sweet.

GINGKO: Widens blood vessels and therefore increases blood flow to the genitals.

HONEY: Offered by the Egyptians to fertility god Min; is still used in some cultures as part of a wedding ceremony.

ICE CREAM: Melting, dripping, creamy, and sweet.

JUICES: Pure fruit and vegetable juices can cleanse the body of toxins.

KAVA KAVA: This amazing plant with its heart-shaped leaves is known to be excellent for reducing stress.

LICORICE: Found by the Chicago Smell and Taste Treatment and Research Foundation to significantly increase blood flow to the penis when combined with the smell of donut.

MASTIC TREE: An evergreen with red or black berries. The ancient Arabic love manual *The Perfumed Garden* advises readers to "take fruit of the mastic tree (*derou*), pound them and macerate them with oil and honey; then drink of the liquid first thing in the morning: you will thus become vigorous for the coitus, and there will be abundance of sperm produced."

NUTMEG: In India, mixed with honey and a half-boiled egg, then taken one hour before lovemaking.

OYSTERS: Probably the most famous of the aphrodisiac foods. Erotic in both taste and appearance (a bit like a woman's genitals). Also full of zinc, a mineral vital in the production of healthy sperm.

PINE NUTS: Used to increase sexual potency since Roman times. According to *The Perfumed Garden* (see M entry),

"He who feels that he is weak for coition should drink before going to bed a glassful of very thick honey and eat twenty almonds and one hundred grains of the pine tree."

QUINCE: Sweet and fragrant. Believed to be the forbidden fruit that tempted Eve in the Garden of Eden.

ROSEMARY: Thought to increase blood flow and therefore heighten sensitivity to touch.

SPANISH FLY: Made from the dried-out bodies of beetles; works by "stimulating" the urinary track; can be dangerous.

TOMATOES: In nineteenth-century France, tomatoes became known as *pommes d'amour* or "love-apples."

UNAGI: Made from sea eel; thought to restore strength.

VANILLA: Comes from the native Mexican orchid and has been considered an aphrodisiac for centuries.

WALNUTS: Thrown at weddings by ancient Romans, who believed they held aphrodisiac powers.

XANAT: Also known as the "Vanilla Orchid"; named after the daughter of the Mexican fertility goddess who loved a Totonac youth. Not being able to marry the boy because of her divine status, she turned herself into the vanilla orchid so that she could always belong to her human beloved and to spread "pleasure and happiness" throughout mankind.

YOHIMBINE: Extracted from Yohimbine bark, it increases blood flow. Should be taken in moderation.

ZINC: Directly related to sperm quality and therefore fertility.

ROMEO AND JULIET

WILLIAM SHAKESPEARE, 1564–1616

ACT 1, SCENE 5

A hall in Capulet's house, at a party.
Romeo has just seen Juliet for the first time

ROMEO:

O, she doth teach the torches to burn bright!
It seems she hangs upon the cheek of night
Like a rich jewel in an Ethiop's ear;
Beauty too rich for use, for earth too dear!
So shines a snow-white swan trooping with crows,
As this fair lady o'er her fellows shows.
The measure done, I'll watch her place of stand,
And, touching hers, make blessed my rude hand.
Did my heart love till now? Forswear it, sight!
I never saw true beauty till this night.

COCKNEY RHYMING SLANG

ENGLISH	TO	SLANG
Eyes		Mince Pies
Face		Boat Race
		EG: *I don't like the look of her boat race.*
Feel		Jellied Eel
Hair		Barnet Fair
		EG: *"His Barnet was a complete mess"*
Heart		Horse and Cart *or* Jam Tart
Kiss		Hit and Miss
Love		Turtle Dove
Love		Rubber Glove
Lover		Danny Glover
Mrs		Love and Kisses *or* Plates and Dishes
Old Man (husband)		Pot and Pan
		EG: *I can't stay, I've got to get back to the pot.*
Undies		Eddie Grundies
Wife		Bread Knife *or* Carving Knife *or* Trouble and Strife

SLANG	TO	ENGLISH
Alan Whickers		Knickers
Brace and Bits		Tits
Bread Knife		Wife
Bristol Cities		Titties

SLANG TO	ENGLISH
Carving Knife	Wife
Cash and Carried	Married
Deaf and Dumb	Bum
Donald Trump	Hump
Duchess of Fife	Wife
Edinburgh Fringe	Minge
Elizabeth Regina	Vagina
Filter Tips	Lips
Ham and Eggs	Legs
Hampton Wick	Prick
Hat with a Bobble	Gobble *(oral sex)*
Hit and Miss	Kiss
Horse and Cart *or* Jam Tart	Heart
Jack the Ripper	Stripper
Khyber Pass	Arse
Love and Kisses *or* Plates and Dishes	Mrs.
Mars and Venus	Penis
Niagara Falls	Balls *(testicles)*
Ocean Pearl	Girl
Oedipus Rex	Sex
Ottis Redding	Wedding
Raspberry Ripple	Nipple
Rubber Glove *or* Turtle Dove	Love
Threepenny Bits	Tits
Trouble and Strife	Wife

Love is Nature's second sun.
>>—George Chapman, *All Fools,* c. 1599

Love is the salt of life.
>>—John Sheffield, *Ode on Love,* 1721

Love is the child of illusion and the parent of disillusion.
>>—Miguel de Unamuno, *Tragic Sense of Life,* 1913

Love is like any other luxury. You have no right to it unless you can afford it.
>>—Anthony Trollope, *The Way We Live Now,* 1875

Love is the tyrant of the heart.
>>—John Ford, *The Lover's Melancholy,* 1628

Love is a kind of anxious fear.
>>—Ovid, *Heroides,* c. 10 B.C.

Love is like those shabby hotels in which all the luxury is in the lobby.
>>—Paul Jean Toulet, *Le Carnet de M. du Paur, homme public,* 1898

In love, pain and pleasure are always at war.
>>—Publilius Syrus, *Sententiae,* c. 43 B.C.

Love is like the measles; we all have to go through it.
> —Jerome K. Jerome, *Idle Thoughts of an
> Idle Fellow—On Being in Love,* 1886

We are all born for love; it is the principle of existence and its only end.
> —Benjamin Disraeli, *Sybil,* 1845

One hour of downright love is worth an age of dully living on.
> —Aphra Behn, *The Rover,* 1680

Love rules the court, the camp, the grove,
And men below, and saints above;
For love is heaven, and heaven is love.
> —Sir Walter Scott, *The Lay of the Last Minstrel,*
> 1805

Marriage is three parts love and seven parts forgiveness of sins.
> —Langdon Mitchell, *The New York Idea,* 1907

HOW TO CHOOSE A MATE,
ACCORDING TO YOUR SKULL

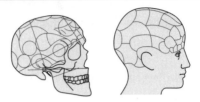

From the book *Love, Courtship, and Marriage, Phrenologically considered. With Useful Hints How to Make a Wise Choice, and Thus Live Happily through Life,* by Professor Blackburne, 1881.

In order to secure true reciprocity of feeling and union of soul, and thus obtain the largest amount of happiness in the married state, select a companion whose phrenological development and temperament for the most part resemble your own, avoiding extremes; do this and you are safe, and you will be happy; but fail to do this and you marry sorrow and regret. An intelligent and well experienced phrenologist will tell you the true character of your intended, and by a careful examination of both heads would be able to show wherein each is adapted to the other, or discover their want of adaptation. How many thousands miss their way, and whose married life is rendered perfectly wretched for want of such help and guidance. Hundreds of the very cleverest men and the most amiable and accomplished women have been rendered miserable through life by the unwise choice they have made, that might have been the happiest of the happy, with a little knowledge of phrenology and a wise determination to be guided by its teaching.

WELSH LOVE SPOONS

The Welsh custom of giving "love spoons" as a romantic gesture from boy to girl began as early as the sixteenth century. From a single piece of wood, men would fashion elaborate designs to show off their carving skills. Symbols in those designs would spell out a young man's desires to his beloved.

Chain	Together forever
Diamond	Wealth or good luck
Heart	I love you
Cross	Faith
Key/keyhole	You hold the key to my heart or security—I'll look after you.
Flower	Affection
Links or beads	Represents the number of children wanted
Knot	Eternal love
Twisted stem	Two lives becoming one
Bell	Let's get married.
Wheel or spade	I'll work for you.

WHAT DAY OF THE WEEK TO MARRY, ACCORDING TO OLD ENGLISH RHYME

Monday for wealth.

Tuesday for health.

Wednesday the best day of all.

Thursday for losses.

Friday for crosses.

Saturday for no luck at all.

GREEK FOR LOVE

In the ancient Greek language, there were several ways to describe love:

GREEK	ENGLISH	WHAT KIND OF LOVE
ερως	Eros	Physical love and attraction
φιλεω	Philos	To feel the love between friends
αγαπη	Agape	Affectionate nonsexual love
στεργω	Stergo	Described the love between parents and children and between close relatives

Many English words are derived from these:

GREEK	ENGLISH	MEANING
αγαπητος	agapetos	beloved
αστοργος	astorgos	without love, heartless
φιλαδελφια	philadelphia	brotherly love
φιλανθρωπια	philanthropia	love of mankind, benevolence
φιλημα	philema	a kiss
φιλια	philia	friendship, affection
φιλοστοργος	philostorgos	loving affectionately

MONTHS TO MARRY,
ACCORDING TO OLD ENGLISH RHYME

VERSION 1

Married when the year is new,
He'll be loving, kind and true.
When February birds do mate
You wed nor dread your fate.
If you wed when March winds blow
Joy and sorrow both you'll know.
Marry in April when you can
Joy for maiden and the man.
Marry in the month of May
And you'll surely rue the day.
Marry when the June roses grow
Over land and sea you'll go.
Those who in July do wed
Must labour for their daily bread.
Whoever wed in August be,
Many a change is sure to see.
Marry in September's shine,
Your living will be rich and fine.
If in October you do marry
Love will come, but riches tarry.
If you wed in bleak November
Only joys will come, remember
When December's snows fall fast,
Marry and true love will last.

VERSION 2

Married in January's roar and rime,
Widowed you'll be before your prime.
Married in February's sleepy weather,
Life you'll tread in time together.
Married when March winds shrill and roar,
Your home will lie on a distant shore.
Married 'neath April's changeful skies,
A checkered path before you lies.
Married when bees o'er May blossoms flit,
Strangers around your board will sit.
Married in month of roses June,
Life will be one long honeymoon.
Married in July with flowers ablaze,
Bitter-sweet memories in after days.
Married in August's heat and drowse,
Lover and friend in your chosen spouse.
Married in September's golden glow,
Smooth and serene your life will go.
Married when leaves in October thin,
Toil and hardships for you begin.
Married in veils of November mist,
Fortune your wedding ring has kissed.
Married in days of December's cheer,
Love's star shines brighter from year to year.

"I was born when she kissed me. I died when she left me.
I lived a few weeks while she loved me."
——Humphrey Bogart as Dixon Steele in
In a Lonely Place (1950)

"I love that you get cold when it is 71 degrees out. I love that
it takes you an hour and a half to order a sandwich. I love that
you get a little crinkle in your nose when you're looking at me
like I'm nuts. I love that after I spend the day with you, I can
still smell your perfume on my clothes. And I love that you are
the last person I want to talk to before I go to sleep at night.
And it's not because I'm lonely, and it's not because it's New
Year's Eve. I came here tonight because when you realize you
want to spend the rest of your life with somebody, you want
the rest of your life to start as soon as possible."
——Billy Crystal as Harry to Meg Ryan as Sally in
When Harry Met Sally . . . (1989)

"It's not the quantity of your sexual relations that counts, it's
the quality. On the other hand, if the quantity drops below
once every eight months, I would definitely look into it."
——Woody Allen as Boris Grushenko in
Love and Death (1975)

"No, I don't think I will kiss you. Although you need kissing badly. That's what's wrong with you. You should be kissed, and often—and by someone who knows how."

> —Clark Gable as Rhett to Vivien Leigh as Scarlett
> in *Gone with the Wind* (1939)

"What is it you want, Mary? What do you want? You . . . you want the moon? Just say the word and I'll throw a lasso around it and pull it down. Hey! That's a pretty good idea! I'll give you the moon, Mary."

> —Jimmy Stewart as George Bailey to Donna Reed
> as Mary in *It's a Wonderful Life* (1946)

"Jerry, don't let's ask for the moon. We have the stars."

> —Bette Davis as Charlotte Vale to Paul Henreid
> as Jerry in *Now Voyager* (1942)

"This is very unusual. I've never been alone with a man before, even with my dress on. With my dress off, it's *most* unusual."

> —Audrey Hepburn as Princess Ann
> ("Anya Smith") to Gregory Peck as Joe Bradley
> in *Roman Holiday* (1953)

"John, when you're kissing me, don't talk about plumbing."

> —Barbara Stanwyck as Elizabeth Lane in
> *Christmas in Connecticut* (1945)

WORDS FOR PARTICULAR KINDS OF LOVE

THE LOVE OF . . .	IS DEFINED AS . . .
cats	*ailurophilia*
England or English people	*Anglophilia*
taking off your clothes	*apodysophilia*
astronomy	*astrophilia*
books or reading	*bibliophilia*
gold	*chrysophilia*
beds	*clinophilia*
trees	*dendrophilia*
work	*ergophilia*
France or French people	*Francophilia/Gallophilia*
Germany or Germans	*Germanophilia*
horses	*hippophilia*
Japan or the Japanese	*Japanophilia*
words	*logophilia*
darkness	*lygophilia*
forests	*nemophilia*
new things	*neophilia*
wine	*oenophilia*
snakes	*ophiophilia*
women	*philogyny*
beards	*pogonophilia*
Russia or the Russians	*Russophilia*
Scotland or the Scots	*Scotophilia*
China or the Chinese	*Sinophilia*
the sea	*thalassophilia*
cheese	*turophilia*

"How bold one gets when one is sure of being loved."

"We are never so defenseless against suffering as when we love, never so helplessly unhappy as when we have lost our love object or its love."

"When a love relationship is at its height there is no room left for any interest in the environment; a pair of lovers are sufficient to themselves."

"Dogs love their friends and bite their enemies, quite unlike people who are incapable of pure love and always have to mix love and hate."

"Whoever loves becomes humble. Those who love have, so to speak, pawned a part of their narcissism."

"Sexual love is undoubtedly one of the chief things in life, and the union of mental and bodily satisfaction in the enjoyment of love is one of its culminating peaks. Apart from a few queer fanatics, all the world knows this and conducts its life accordingly. Science alone is too delicate to admit it."

1   Behold, thou art fair, my love; behold, thou art fair; thou hast doves' eyes within thy locks: thy hair is as a flock of goats, that appear from mount Gilead.

2   Thy teeth are like a flock of sheep that are even shorn, which came up from the washing; whereof every one bear twins, and none is barren among them.

3   Thy lips are like a thread of scarlet, and thy speech is comely: thy temples are like a piece of a pomegranate within thy locks.

4   Thy neck is like the tower of David builded for an armory, whereon there hang a thousand bucklers, all shields of mighty men.

5   Thy two breasts are like two young roes that are twins, which feed among the lilies.

6   Until the daybreak, and the shadows flee away, I will get me to the mountain of myrrh, and to the hill of frankincense.

7   Thou art all fair, my love; there is no spot in thee.

8   Come with me from Lebanon, my spouse, with me from Lebanon: look from the top of Amana, from the top of Shenir and Hermon, from the lions' dens, from the mountains of the leopards.

9   Thou hast ravished my heart, my sister, my spouse; thou hast ravished my heart with one of thine eyes, with one chain of thy neck.

10   How fair is thy love, my sister, my spouse! how much better is thy love than wine! and the smell of thine ointments than all spices!

11   Thy lips, O my spouse, drop as the honeycomb: honey and milk are under thy tongue; and the smell of thy garments is like the smell of Lebanon.

12   A garden inclosed is my sister, my spouse; a spring shut up, a fountain sealed.

13   Thy plants are an orchard of pomegranates, with pleasant fruits; camphire, with spikenard,

14   Spikenard and saffron; calamus and cinnamon, with all trees of frankincense; myrrh and aloes, with all the chief spices —

15   A fountain of gardens, a well of living waters, and streams from Lebanon.

16   Awake, O north wind; and come, thou south; blow upon my garden, that the spices thereof may flow out. Let my beloved come into his garden, and eat his pleasant fruits.

MY FUNNY VALENTINE

BY RICHARD RODGERS AND LORENZ HART

My funny valentine
Sweet comic valentine,
You make me smile with my heart
Your looks are laughable,
Unphotographable
Yet you're my favorite work of art.

Is your figure less than Greek
Is your mouth a little weak,
When you open it to speak
Are you smart?

But don't change a hair for me
Not if you care for me,
Stay little valentine stay
Each day is Valentine's Day.

Is your figure less than Greek
Is your mouth a little weak,
When you open it to speak
Are you smart?

But don't you change one hair for me
Not if you care for me,
Stay little valentine stay
Each day is Valentine's Day.

FAMOUS WEDDINGS AND
THEIR LOCATIONS

COUPLE	LOCATION	DATE
Wallis Simpson & the Duke of Windsor	Chateau de Cande, France	June 3, 1937
Clark Gable & Carole Lombard	First Methodist Episcopal Church, Kingman, Arizona	March 29, 1939
Lucille Ball & Desi Arnaz	Byram River Beagle Club, Greenwich, Connecticut	November 30, 1940
Lauren Bacall & Humphrey Bogart	Farmhouse in Lucas, Ohio	May 21, 1945
Rita Hayworth & Prince Aly Khan	Town Hall, Cannes, France	May 27, 1949
John F. Kennedy & Jaqueline Bouvier	St. Mary's Church, Newport, Rhode Island	September 12, 1953
Marilyn Monroe & Joe DiMaggio	City Hall, San Francisco, California	January 14, 1954
Audrey Hepburn & Mel Ferrer	Burgenstock, Switzerland	September 25, 1954
Grace Kelly & Prince Rainier, III	Cathedral of St. Nicholas, Monaco	April 19, 1956
John Lennon & Yoko Ono	British Consulate, Gibraltar	March 20, 1969
Mick Jagger & Bianca Perez	St. Anne's Chapel, St. Tropez, France	May 12, 1971
Trudie Styler & Sting	11th Century Chapel, Wiltshire, England	August 22, 1992
John F. Kennedy Jr. & Carolyn Bessette	First African Baptiste Church, Cumberland Island, Georgia	September 21, 1996

P. A. I. R.* PROJECT FINDINGS

Couples who fall in love more slowly are less in love and less satisfied as newlyweds.

The more quickly partners fall in love, the shorter their courtship, the more rapidly their commitment escalates, and the fewer the number of downturns they experience.

The more quickly partners become sexually involved, the shorter their courtship, the more rapidly their commitment escalates, and the fewer the number of downturns they experience.

The more couples reportedly experience conflict, the longer their courtship lasts, the slower their commitment accelerates, and the more downturns they experience.

The course of courtship—particularly the rate at which the couple's commitment accelerates—is more closely aligned with men's than women's psychological orientations toward their partners.

Newly married wives' satisfaction with their ability to visit with friends and relatives as well as their ability to spend time with their husbands is associated with their marital satisfaction.

Wives' satisfaction with their sexual relationship is associated with their marital satisfaction during the second year of marriage.

---

*P. A. I. R. is the Processes of Adaptation in Intimate Relationships Project, conceived in 1979 at Pennsylvania State University.

Wives' satisfaction with their ability to influence their spouse is associated with their marital satisfaction during the third year of marriage.

Husbands' satisfaction with their ability to influence their spouse is associated with their marital satisfaction during the second year of marriage.

Newly married wives' satisfaction with the amount of time they have to engage in their own leisure activities is associated with their love for their husbands.

Husbands' satisfaction with their sexual relationship is associated with their marital satisfaction during the first year of marriage (and marginally associated with their marital satisfaction during the second and third years of marriage).

Husbands' satisfaction with their finances is marginally associated with their love for their wives during the second year of marriage and is significantly associated with their love during the third year of marriage.

Husbands in dual-earner marriages report higher levels of negative marital interaction than do husbands in single-earner marriages (note, however, that the variability among dual-earner husbands is extensive).

Wives feel less love for their partners than do husbands.

Spouses spend less time talking to each other after a year of marriage.

SYMBOLS OF LOVE

SYMBOL	WHAT IT IS	MEANING
	Love heart	In Christian belief, the heart holds all emotions, especially love.
	Cupid and Cupid's bow and arrow	Cupid was the son of Venus, Roman goddess of love. When someone was shot by one of his love arrows, that person would fall in love with the first person they saw.
	The color red	Red is associated with love and passion, probably because it's the color of blood.
	The rose	The rose is said to be the favorite flower of Venus, Roman goddess of love. The word is also an anagram of EROS, the god of love in Greek mythology.
	Love knots	These are a series of interlacing loops that have no beginning or end, and thus symbolize endless love. Typically drawn on paper or made out of ribbon.
	Two birds, sitting together	African birds known as "love birds" because they sit so closely together in pairs.

COLUMBIA UNIVERSITY, ENGL 3707, ROMANTIC POETRY SYLLABUS

Shelley, "Defense of Poetry"

Coleridge, "Literature and the Fine Arts"

Wordsworth, "Preface to Lyrical Ballads"

Blake, *Marriage of Heaven and Hell*, *The Book of Urizen*

Byron, "Cain"

Shelley, *The Cenci*

Wordsworth, Selected lyrics, Prospectus to *The Recluse*, from *The Prelude*, "Michael"

Coleridge, "Kubla Khan," "Fears in Solitude," "France," "An Ode, The Nightingale"

Byron, *Don Juan*, Cantos 2–4

Keats, "The Eve of St, Agnes," "Ode on a Grecian Urn," "Ode to a Nightingale," "To Autumn"

SAYINGS PRINTED ON
NECCO SWEETHEARTS CANDIES

Be Mine

Be True

Be Good

I Love You

Marry Me

Sweet Talk

☺

Dig Me

Groovy

Let's Kiss

Got Love

Love You

Hug Me

First Kiss

Sure Love

Look Good

Dream

Amore

Romeo

Angel

Swing Time

In The Mood

Much Ado

Nice Girl

Girl Power

Time Out

1-800-CUPID

You Rock

Love Is Sweet

Call Me

Fax Me

Write Me

Email Me

Page Me

Awesome

Cool Dude

You Go Girl

Yeah Right

Love Me Tender

I Got U Babe

Let It

My Way

URA Star

Venus

Odyssey

Rising Star

Dress Up

Ask Me

Diva

Vogue

In Style

Tres Chic

That Smile

What's Up

URA QT

Two Hearts

Te Amo

Teach Me

School Mate

Whiz Kid

Love Letter

Book Club

Pen Pal

Class Act

Let's Read

3 Wishes

Charm Me

Ever After

New You

Magic

IM Me

#1 Fan

Dream Team

Cheer Me On

Fit for Love

Be a Sport

Be My Hero

Heart of Gold

All Star

Love My Team

Love Life

My Man

Thank You

For You

Cutie Pie

Miss You

Love Her

Love Him

UR Kind

I Hope

Dream Girl

Smile

My Girl

from *The Compact Oxford English Dictionary*

noun 1 an intense feeling of deep affection. **2** a deep romantic or sexual attachment to someone. **3** a great interest and pleasure in something. **4** a person or thing that one loves. **5** (in tennis, squash, etc.) a score of zero. apparently from the phrase *play for love* (i.e. the love of the game, not for money).

verb 1 feel love for. **2** like very much. **3 loving** showing love or great care.

— PHRASES **love me, love my dog** proverb if you love someone, you must accept everything about them, even their faults or weaknesses. **make love 1** have sexual intercourse. **2 make love to** (dated) pay amorous attention to. **there's no love lost between** there is mutual dislike between.

— DERIVATIVES **loveless** adjective **lovingly** adverb.

— ORIGIN *Old English,* related to LEAVE 2 and LIEF.

ACKNOWLEDGMENTS

First, we are truly grateful to our husbands, without whom we would not have had the inspiration to pull this together. To Jonathan Gale, Dan Duane, and Martin Gammon, we say a huge thank you.

Al Alvarez provided his literary expertise for this project, and his patience and suggestions are so greatly appreciated.

We are also deeply indebted to many others who have been coerced into providing help, support and ideas: Kate Alvarez, Rebecca Berger, Caroline Bondy, Ivo Bondy, Jessica Bondy, Rosemary Bondy, Rupert Bondy, Shuna Black, Becca Chicot, Nicolas Cobbin, Kris Dahl, Ali Dillon, Kelly Duane, Nicola Gammon, Kate Humble, Emma de Lotz, Ben Maniatis, Chris Maniatis, Elizabeth Maniatis, Kathleen Maniatis, Nick Maniatis, Patricia Maniatis, Ted Maniatis, Theo Maniatis, Natasha Plowright, Colleen Shelly, Derk Shelly, Edwina Silver, Lesley Thorne, Henry Singer, Debbie Weil, Doug Weil, Judy Weil, Ken Wlaschin, and Mo Wlaschin.

SOURCES

P. 18 Excerpts from *Casablanca* granted courtesy of Warner Bros. Entertainment Inc. P. 19 Image courtesy of Lucy Brown, Rutgers University. P. 31 Sternberg, R. J. (1997). "Construct validation of a triangular love scale." *European Journal of Social Psychology*, 27, 313–335. P. 43 BRIDE'S Millennium Report: Wedding Love & Money. P. 46: Sternberg, R. J. (1998). *Love Is a Story*. New York: Oxford University Press. P. 57 "The Dove Report: Challenging Beauty," April 2004. P. 58 "Tongue" by Zbigniew Herbert. Published in *Selected Poems*, Penguin Books, 1968, translated by Czeslaw Milosz and Peter Dale Scott; translation copyright Milosz & Scott, Penguin 1968. P. 59 *Marriage and the Economy : Theory and Evidence from Advanced Industrial Societies*, Shoshana A. Grossbard-Schectman (editor), Cambridge University Press, 2003. P. 61 "Hormonal changes when falling in love," Donatella Marazziti and Domenico Canale, University of Pisa, Italy, *Psychoneuroendocrinology* (2004), Aug 29 (7):931–6. P. 66 RWA from Book Industry Study Group and American Bookseller Association reports, and from tallies in Ingram's catalogue of all book releases. P. 68 Score Networks and Online Publishers Association. P. 78 "Patterns and Universals of Mate Poaching across 53 Regions," David P. Schmitt and 121 Members of the International Sexual Description Project, *Journal of Personality and Social Psychology* 2004, Vol. 86, No. 4, 560–584. Pp. 69 and 83 U.S. Census Bureau, Annual Social and Economic Supplement: 2003 Current Population Survey, Current Population Reports, Series P20–553, "America's Families and Living Arrangements: 2003" and earlier reports. Pp. 90–92 AVERT.org. P. 94 From The American Film Institute's 100 Years . . . 100 Passions, America's Greatest Love Stories. P. 106 From the book *Love, Courtship, and Marriage, Phrenologically considered. With Useful hints how to make a wise choice, and thus live happily through life*, by Professor Blackburne, 1881. P. 118 Words by Lorenz Hart, Music by Richard Rodgers. © 1937 Chappell & Co Inc, USA, Warner/Chappell North America Ltd, London W6 8BS Reproduced by permission of International Music Publications Ltd. All Rights Reserved. P. 120: THE PAIR Project, University of Texas at Austin, principal investigator: Ted L. Huston. P. 126 *Compact Oxford English Dictionary,* Second Edition, Oxford University Press, 2003.